RELEASE The POWER of Re³

Review, Redo & Renew
for
Positive Change & Transformation

Susan YOUNG

Library of Congress-in-Publication-Data: 2017912689
Young, Susan
Release the Power of Re3: Review, Redo & Renew for Positive Change and Transformation by Susan Young

Published by ReNew You Ventures
Editing by Elizabeth Dixon and Judy Dippel
Book Design by Kendra Cagle, www.5LakesDesign.com
Cover Photos by Sarah Sandell, Sarah Leslie Photography
ISBN-10: 0-9985561-0-6
ISBN-13: 978-0-9985561-0-9

This book is dedicated to

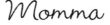
Nick & Ally

Your love, loyalty, support, and wisdom are powerful beyond words in my heart and in my life. You are the fruits of my spirit. May you always have the power to tap into your possibilities and live extraordinary lives.

I love you both forever and always,

Momma

What People are Saying

*"Susan Young makes the process of positive change
and transformation very simple. If you feel the need for self-
improvement, this book is for you. If you want to sharpen your mind
and be more deliberate in your actions to your road to success, this
book is for you. I had the pleasure of meeting Susan Young during a
brief flight to my destination and Release the Power of Re3 is truly an
extension of her and her desire to share with the world an improved
way to think and be. I highly recommend this book to you. It is an
easy digest and very applicable to your everyday life."*

—Floyd McLendon, Jr.

*"What a wonderfully concise book. Susan Young gives personal life
examples to help us take a deeper look into our own lives. Quick
definitions, examples and stories followed with questions designed
to provoke thought and introspection. Well written, personal and
helpful for peeling back the layers of the onion in allowing us to
release our own power and potential. A chapter a day
keeps the negativity away!"*

—Katie Cappozzo

*"Both practical and inspirational, this book can serve as your go-to
manual for successfully adapting to life changes and creating new
ways of being and doing for a fulfilling life. Broken down into small
but pithy kernels of tested and true wisdom based on author Susan
C. Young's own personal life experiences, the book can be read,
internalized, and applied just a few pages at a time. Susan shares
the raw and moving real-life events that led to her writing this book.*

Readable and fun, Release the Power of Re3 is a powerful and effective tool for people across all demographics, and an excellent resource for both personal and professional shift and expansion. I would recommend this book for anyone who is in the midst of life-altering changes, even trauma, as well as for organizations whose team members/staff are facing transitions or need an infusion of fresh perspectives and motivation."

—Elizabeth C. Dixon

"Excellent! It's the perfect formula for moving your life in the right direction!"

—Brian Cullen

"What a powerful and important book for anyone who is ready to shed the negativity and embrace the life they've always wanted. I loved it! 5/5 stars"

—Shelly

"Life is full of change, good and bad. Susan Young has created a powerful guide that not only helps us navigate difficult changes in our lives, but empowers us to make changes where needed. I found it full of wisdom, inspiration, and actionable ideas I can take to make a difference in my life. I also loved the way the book is laid out in three main sections - Review, Redo, & Renew. It's the kind of book that I will pick up and page through on those days I need motivation and guidance. If you like short, easy to digest nuggets that will energize you to take charge of your l ife, you will want to keep this book by your bedside."

—Tina Hallis

"Wow to this fun and profound read! Susan Young is a treasure. She is full of positive energy which she freely shares with whomever she is with. Susan came into my life at a much-needed time and her book helped me get through a difficult time where I was second guessing decisions I had made. I love the overriding theme that your past does not have to define who you are or dictate where you are going. We have an unlimited opportunity to change our mindsets, reset, and do over for different and more positive outcomes. We just need to release the power :) Read this book now and get on with your transformation already!"

—Tammie Kovacs

"Susan teaches from her heart and past tough experiences. I'm always looking for positive, easy, and quick reading tools that inspire and motivate me to try a new behavior. Susan gives us "wisdom on how to rethink it, redo it, and reconnect with yourself and others." It's perfect for however much time you have to read and restart the direction of your fabulous life."

—Deborah Mann

"Absolutely love the energy that vibrates from this book! Release the Power of Re3 is a quick read that really allows you to take a peek at all of the small things in your life that need a (re)boot! Thank you for writing this!"

—Britney

"RE" such a simple prefix that offers such possibility. Susan C. Young's Release the Power of Re3 reminds us that change is possible. Whether a professional change as so many experience today in downsizing or the personal change of a divorce, we can find power

in RE. Susan has given us 77 ways to think about how our lives can be different. I appreciated her quotes and her anecdotes to guide my thinking about reinvention, recreation, and Renewing my life. Great, easy, and accessible read for anyone wanting to see their life a little bit differently.

—Mary H. Conroy

"I read a little of this book at my friend's house and realized I had to get my OWN copy....it really speaks to the heart!"

—Ann Marie

"Susan Young is one of the kindest and most amazing people I've ever met. Her book is what she lives, acts, and does written on paper. Amazing book, and I wouldn't expect anything less from her."

—Leisha Hallis

"Susan has a unique talent to speak to your heart through the pages of this book. I felt as if I was having tea next to a friend who was sharing her infinite wisdom with me. No matter what was going on, I could just pick up this book and she would help clarify my world in just moments with simple, easy to apply, small chapters. I keep a copy on my table so that my visitors can enjoy the gift of peace that she has given me!"

—Natalie Leon

Contents

1st Power
Review

Redo

3rd Power

Renew

.

$\mathcal{F}$oreword

By Mark LeBlanc

In your hands you hold a remarkable book written by a spirited author. Susan Young is rare indeed. In fact, her enthusiasm is contagious. We live in a world of challenge and change. No matter what season of life you are living, you now have a guiding set of principles that can light your way through the ups and downs of life and work.

Many people hold on tightly to achievements of long ago instead of expanding on those achievements and setting new goals. Far more carry forward the mistakes of their past, decisions they wish they could change, and regrets that harden their hearts.

Susan has given you the keys to reset your counters to zero and let go of the good, bad, ugly and great of your past. Let today be the dividing line in the sand and you will create a new chapter of ideas, goals, experiences, and moments that matter.

Regardless of what has gone before you, you can unlock a new combination for living a life on purpose and by design, not by accident. It will require serious reflection and heavy lifting. You are worth it. You will have new results to celebrate and the rewards will be priceless.

Always remember, no change—no change.

After reading Susan's book, answering questions and coming up with new answers, your life will never be the same. In fact, keep her book handy and reread over and over. Make it your desktop or bedside companion and it will serve you well. Refer to it often and it will keep you on path or help you get back on path if you go off on a tangent disguised as an opportunity.

One wish I have for you is to hear her speak. You will meet a force for good in this world. I am fortunate to call Susan my friend.

I leave you with a single word. It is my gift to you and represents so much of what I have learned and been reminded of in this special book. It is Latin for "Keep Going." I want you to remember this word for the rest of your life.

Ultreia!

—Mark LeBlanc
Speaker, Pilgrim, and Author of *Never Be the Same*
and *Growing Your Business*

Welcome

Thank you for picking up this book. Readers tell me that it is both fun and dynamic. You will find it to be a quick read filled with game-changing ideas. These can be implemented immediately to change the direction of your life—for the better!

As a professional keynote speaker and workshop leader, I have the profound honor of touching people's lives around the world. It is my greatest desire to empower audiences with tools which have the power to transform—not only their professional lives, but their personal lives as well. We know the various parts of our lives are not exclusive from one another; rather, they are integrated moving parts which are essential for creating a whole, happy, and well-balanced person and life.

When Audiences Experience My Programs, They Gain:

1. More positivity, optimism, and motivation for achieving their goals at work and in life.
2. Inspired ideas for transforming personal and professional relationships.
3. Take-away tools to enhance their education, effectiveness, and confidence.
4. A shifted mindset for how to best survive, thrive, and happily arrive—in times of change.

It is my sincere hope that
Release the Power of Re^3
will do the same for you!

How Re³ Came to Be

Ask yourself:

- *Would you like to create real and positive change in your life?*
- *Are there areas where you desire to improve?*
- *Do you feel stuck, but unsure of how to get moving forward?*
- *Are you facing unpalatable changes which you never imagined you would face?*
- *Do you set goals or make plans on a regular basis which flounder, falter, fail, or never come to fruition?*

Your life doesn't have to be lived in fear, disappointment, and frustration. Expect to be refreshed as you discover more about yourself, chapter-by-chapter—and because today is a brand-new day. I'm delighted that you are about to learn to live in a more positive, powerful, and satisfying way.

Regardless of what has happened in your past, you can optimize your present moment with proven strategies to guide you as you begin again and start anew.

*"The secret of change is to focus all of your energy not on
fighting the old, but on building the new."*
—Socrates

What About My Life?

I want you to know that I am not asserting my program or strategies in this book lightly or from a place of naiveté, simple "rah-rah" enthusiasm, or unbridled positivity. Without having experienced hard times myself, I would not now have the enriched insight needed to teach others how to move toward better times.

Rather, I know what I share within this book to be true because I have lived it and I intimately understand how unwelcomed change can rock your world. I walk the talk with sincerity, humility, compassion, and gratitude. I hope that by sharing my story with you, you too will find hope for renewal and resilience—that you will find untapped strength and a new lightness and joy as you walk through to the other side successfully, whatever the change you face.

Over a short period of only a few years, my children and I endured extraordinary and significant challenges and changes. A perfect storm of terrible events and situations unfolded: alcoholism, arrest, unemployment, divorce, cancer, deaths of family members, economic loss and uncertainty, a law suit, single motherhood, multiple moves, and the attendant debilitating emotions of fear of the unknown and unresolved grief.

My husband's alcoholism led to his getting a DUI which resulted in his immediate termination from a prosperous twenty-year career. He never recovered and never worked again, and our twenty-three-year marriage soon ended in heartbreaking divorce. Not too long afterward, I found him dead. My children and I were devastated by the tragic loss of this intelligent and loving good man who succumbed to a debilitating disease. During this same period, my father suffered with a cancer that eventually took his life. As a single mother, I juggled the duties of a one-parent household while I watched my teenage children grieve the loss of their father. Additionally, as the U.S. economy was crumbling between 2008 and 2012, our life savings and investments went up in smoke. Dare I mention that our home even became infested with mold, mice, and moths in the midst of our other troubles?

Stressors continued due to multiple moves and home renovations. As my son enlisted in the military during wartime immediately out of high school and my daughter moved to Hawaii with her new husband, I abruptly became an empty nester. The family life I cherished became unrecognizable in a new reality where nothing felt stable or secure.

It might have been less painful and easier to navigate if we had had to deal with only one change at a time. However, changes kept coming in clusters and from all directions. As a small family of three, we did the best we could to move forward with courage, grace, and dignity. You can only imagine the amount of doubt, second-guessing, and regret that one experiences when having to make important life decisions under so much duress from multiple sources.

Throughout these challenges there was still joy to be found— making it all the more precious. I soon went back to college to earn my Master's Degree and graduated Suma Cum Laude. I fell in love with a wonderful man who fell in love with my children and me. Even though he lived a thousand miles away and we had to commute to be together until the children graduated from high school, he remained steadfast and loyal until we could build a life together.

It is with great empathy born of experience that I say, *we all do the best we can with what we have and what we know,* but there is always a margin for error. When our life becomes unrecognizable from what we once knew it to be, most of us have no idea how to build again—or even where to start. Even the most positive person is tested. This certainly was true for me.

Move forward with me several years. My kids are now young adults living independent and fulfilling lives. I have built a new life, am a grandmother, and am enjoying this new chapter. As a devoted mother, however, there remains a residue of heartache and regret in a part of me that wishes things could have been different. The question of *what if?* lingers.

As you will read in Chapter 9, "Readdressing," my kids recently requested a serious heart-to-heart conversation with me to talk about what had happened during our family changes over those challenging years. The talk helped all three of us gain clarity, peace, and forgiveness. In addition to our game-changing, straight-on and frank conversation, something miraculous and unexpected occurred.

Readdressing how we each felt about the past allowed me to release burdens in my heart which had been suppressing my spirit and blocking my joy. My now adult children expressed their perspectives and asked questions of me that deserved answers. With obstructions cleared, my brain opened like a dam bursting. Thoughts and ideas flooded into my mind so quickly that I could barely write them down fast enough. Within less than five hours I had the entire concept, outline with topics, and title for this book—the very one you now hold in your hands.

This Book Found Me

The next morning, I called my dear and brilliant friend Cheri Neal to discuss my inspired "aha" moment. Cheri is not only a fellow speaker and certified life coach, but she is the Zion Township Supervisor in Zion, Illinois. She enthusiastically agreed to discuss each topic with me so that I could generate rapid-fire content through stimulating conversation. Cheri became my writing muse and empowered me to take my writing to the next level.

I took long walks in the rambling woods behind our home. Everyone should have such an office in which to work—I carried along my outline, my voice recorder, and my Samsung Galaxy 7 phone. As I walked among the trees and the falling leaves, this technology allowed me to capture my ideas as fast as they were coming. All of the transcribing was done using the voice recognition software on my cell phone. I would then email the transcripts to myself to copy and paste into my outline upon returning home.

This book found me and demanded to be written. Every author has the book they have to write—this is mine. The entire manuscript was written in one week! It then took another week to rewrite and enrich with research, a week to edit, and a week for the cover design and interior layout to be complete. It's as if I had celestial assistance to ensure I would and could complete the task at hand. I have never known such a zone of unbridled creativity, and I hope you will agree the end result is extraordinary.

Although this book was completed and ready to publish within 30 days of its inception, it brings you 30 years of wisdom which was earned, learned, and lived by example. Every single idea has helped me thrive and be resilient. If you so choose, it will do the same for you.

Truth has Universal Application

You will find that the lessons of truth shared herein can be applied to your life, loves, relationships, goals, and business. Since you will continue to experience changes in every aspect of your life, *Release the Power of Re³* will serve as an excellent reference and companion. Whether you need to process your past, navigate your present, or plan for your future, second chances abound for making things bigger, bolder, and better.

Second Chances

I believe in second chances. What about you? Your past does not have to define, determine, or dictate who you are now or where you are going—especially if you want to create new and improved results.

You have the ability, freedom, and unlimited opportunity to change your direction if you desire. If you are like the rest of 99.99% of the population, there are aspects of your life for which you would like a reset button—a do-over for a different outcome—a new experience, a better method, or an easier way. Let this book guide you.

A Second Chance is Transformational When . . .

- Your current reality does not align with your hopes, dreams, plans, or expectations.
- You are willing to shift your mindset and approach to life from a new perspective.
- You are willing to forgive yourself and others for past pain, regret, and mistakes.
- You seek personal growth and professional development for lifelong learning, fulfillment, and greater prosperity.
- You want to build upon your strengths, talents, and successes to take your life to the next level.

It is a blessing and a gift when other people provide you with a second chance. Now, give yourself permission to do the same for you.

Make the Right Choices for the Right Changes

You are capable of making positive changes to improve and transform life as you now know it. When you *Release the Power of Re³*, you are opening the doors to release innovation, generation, creative problem solving, and exponential ideation.

Whether you hope to create something which is completely brand new or seek to build upon the past and make it even better, this book will help you make the right choices for the right changes.

For some of you, these opening pages may seem unnecessary to read. You may feel impatient and eager to learn the powerful information that you can apply—right away, today! If you must, jump ahead, but after you've read a few chapters, please come back and read these pages. They will help you get the most out of this book.

For others, you will see these next dozen pages as welcome and necessary preparation to fully understand the purpose of *Release the Power of Re³*—which is a proven resource to influence needed change—as you relax and read in your own space.

As you sit safe and secure, away from the stress-filled rat race, I encourage you to enjoy the quiet and allow these next few pages to bring issues to mind that you can expect to change through the help provided in each chapter. These groundwork pages will increase your awareness—perhaps even rid your denial right up front—regarding significant areas that need change. It's all about you—to show you how to release the power and take what may feel impossible and discover that positive change and transformation are more than possible.

The Power of the Prefix 'Re'

Change will happen again, again, and again . . . with you, without you, for you, or against you. That's life.

You may be asking . . . "What the heck is Re^3 ?"

Re is a prefix, which when used in front of a word, changes its meaning to convey a fresh beginning, *a do-over, a repeat, a shift in perspective,* or an opportunity to create something new.

The Prefix 'Re' . . .

1. Means "again" or "again and again" or "do again" to indicate repetition.
2. Represents "back" or "backward" to indicate withdrawal or stepping back.
3. Signifies the return to a previous condition.

With this in mind, you might think of a few action verbs which represent the attitudes, mindsets, decisions, or conditions which have helped make you or others successful in life and in business.

Simply by adding the prefix **Re,** you have *created an opportunity to change what's not working, strengthen what is, and gain the clarity to know the difference.*

When you add the prefix **Re,** you are activating the power of the word within your mind and heart—to head in a new direction to build momentum for positive change and transformation.

Why Re^3?

Re to the ***third power*** was designed to represent the three key categories for sustainable change shared in my book:

1. Review

2. Redo

3. Renew

Within each of these three **Re** categories, you will find specific and strategic action steps which all begin with the Prefix **Re**. When you look at the three dimensions of your past, present, and future changes and apply the **Re³** solutions you will find in this book, you may discover the key for unlocking exponential possibilities in your life.

It is Time to *Release the Power of* Re^3 When . . .

- What you're currently doing isn't working.
- Your heart is burdened by regrets for what would've, could've, or should've been.
- Your results don't match your plans or desires.
- You are faced with major changes and want to respond wisely, proactively, and appropriately.
- You are considering numerous alternatives and need guidance to make the best decisions moving forward.
- Something was originally done wrong and needs to be made right.

- Something is old and tired and needs to be updated.
- You feel stuck and need a catalyst to get going.
- Something is broken and needs to be fixed.
- You want more definitive control over your destiny to create an amazing life.
- You want to release sadness, disappointments, and pain of the past in order to discover happiness, fulfillment, and peace.
- You've achieved a goal and are asking, "What's next?"

As you read my book, stop, step back, and contemplate how you can look at your changes from these three new perspectives: **Review, Redo,** and **Renew.**

Arrange for Change

"You must take personal responsibility. You cannot change the circumstances, the seasons, or the wind, but you can change yourself."
—Jim Rohn

Change is the one constant in your life which you will experience from your first breath to your last. It is a significant word used to describe unlimited scenarios. It can bring you the greatest joy and fulfillment or wreak havoc and destruction. Most changes fall under two categories:

1. ## Planned Change
   The change resulting from a deliberate decision, a planned event, or an expected outcome.
2. ## Unplanned Change
   The change resulting from an unforeseen, unpredictable, or unexpected event. It can be imposed and undesired.

Sometimes the changes in your life are planned with a sound strategy, optimism, and intention. Other changes that come upon you, however, will catch you by surprise, sabotage your success, break your heart, cause you stress, or leave you feeling lost and not your best. Whether you are dealing with *planned* or *unplanned* change, there are always degrees of adaptation and reorientation required to be resilient. How you handle one change might not be relevant or useful for handling another. Different situations call for different solutions.

Your key to thriving is to fortify yourself with the tools, skill sets, and the mindset necessary to respond to change from a position of personal strength, deliberation, and choice. These enable you to be better equipped to shape life on your terms.

The sooner you accept change as an inevitable part of life, the more empowered you will be for resilience and transformation. The sooner you address and improve your attitude about change, and your response to it, the more personal power you will have to navigate pain, struggle, and adversity.

Regardless of your circumstances at work, at home, with teams, in relationships, in your community, or in the world, change is undeniable and ever present—for everyone!

The Three Dimensions of Change

Wouldn't it be great if you had to deal with only one change at a time? Or if all of the changes in your life were planned, desired, or predictable? Not only is that unrealistic, but change is three dimensional:

Your Past—Changes which have already happened.
Your Present—Changes you are currently navigating.
Your Future—Changes which are forthcoming.

The attitudes, beliefs, and meanings you attach to these changes in your life will significantly impact your levels of spiritual, mental, emotional, and even physical well-being. Ask yourself: *Are my responses to change helpful or hurtful?*

Once you "ditch the denial" about your feelings, you will begin to recognize the power of resilience and renewal you were born with. Stop thinking that you have to settle or compromise to merely survive. Become mindful of what is not working, and begin to take the steps needed to change for the better. Simply keep reading.

Constructive Change & Transformation

Change for the sake of change is <u>not</u> what this book is about. This book is filled to the brim with ideas for inspiring change to improve positivity, performance, productivity, profitability, team unity, happiness, relationships, health, knowledge, and serenity.

Every one of the 77 chapters will provide you with a complete concept which is easy to read, process, and apply. While you are not expected to apply all 77, select those which are currently relevant and useful for your life situation. One idea may be irrelevant now, but will resonate to empower you in the future. Whether you capture three golden nuggets or many, I hope they serve you well to *move from life transition to transformation.*

Your Mindset Matters

"People with a growth mindset believe that they can improve with effort. They outperform those with a fixed mindset, even when they have a lower IQ, because they embrace challenges, treating them as opportunities to learn something new."

—Travis Bradberry

Your mindset is the single most important influence on how you respond to change. It can be the *make or break difference* between success or failure, confidence or fear, hope or despair.

Ask yourself: *Do I embrace change or resist it? Is my mindset open and willing to make friends with it?*

In twenty years of speaking, experience, and research, I have found that when people associate change with fun, growth, adventure, variety, opportunity, and possibility, they are more agile and resilient. This kind of mindset is what makes transformation possible.

Exponential Resilience

"Resilience is that ineffable quality that allows some people to be knocked down by life and come back stronger than ever. Rather than letting failure overcome them and drain their resolve, they find a way to rise from the ashes."

—Psychology Today

Throughout your entire life you will experience continuous change. You are not who you were 5, 10, 15, or 20 years ago. Nor will you remain the same into the future.

Once you embrace the continuous change as a natural process for your growth and evolution, you will be reminded that who, what, and where you are now are temporary conditions. Understanding and accepting this fact is foundational for creating positive change and transformation.

Given that every single one of us will experience massive change, why is it that some of us handle it well while others don't? Resilient people don't avoid life's hard knocks; they face them head-on, and find ways to adapt, survive, thrive, and flourish.

Resiliency. . .

- marks the difference between those who can experience adversity and bounce back stronger than ever and those who can't;
- is the process by which people adapt to change or crises;
- is the capability of managing your feelings, impulses, reactions, and emotions.

There are two universal human reactions to change. Which is yours?

Many people walk through the depths of dreadful circumstances and face indignities, abuse, and challenges, it seems, without missing a beat. They find a way to navigate their journeys and emerge on the other side as stronger and wiser people.

There are those, however, who face similar challenges who become discouraged, defeated, depressed, and lose any hope of healing and moving forward, to the point of remaining in a state of "stuck and unhappy."

Granted, life will sometimes bring heartbreaks which seem impossible to reconcile—the death of a child, chronic illness, the end of a marriage, the failure of a business, or the loss of your joy. But if we are to go on living, we have a choice for how we are going to react and respond—***Review, Redo,*** and ***Renew.***

Once you read through this book, and return to it as needed, you will learn methods and tools for being more resilient. You can apply your insights to every aspect of your life, personally and professionally. You will be more empowered to thrive from a position of strength and wisdom.

It is then you will be able to answer the question "Which is yours?" by saying "With resiliency, strength, and wisdom."

1st Power Review

Review

Socrates is known for saying, *"The unexamined life is not worth living."* Successful people at every level and in every walk of life understand that examination and review are essential for achieving their desired outcomes. Most professions require it for delivering service excellence and making informed decisions. For example:

- Accountants review revenues against expenses to ensure the viability of a business.
- Employers hold reviews to evaluate the contribution and performance of employees.
- Doctors review your health at your annual checkup to keep you healthy and vital.
- Teachers review homework, effort, and participation to determine grades.
- Coaches review film footage of games to improve strategies to win the game.
- Business consultants review aspects of an organization to help them improve the culture, engagement, and performance outcomes.
- CEOs review strategic business plans to ensure they're on target for achieving their goals.
- Sales managers review their team's production and closing ratios to ensure profitability.
- Association's review their membership to know how to better serve them.
- Companies review customer satisfaction surveys to decide how they need to improve their products and services.

The importance of reviewing is apparent and proven. However, the majority of people don't do it in their own lives. Do you want to live your best life today?

Take action by beginning to **REVIEW** where you have been, where you are now, and where you would like to be.

Why Review?

1. You will gain clarity on what is working, what is not working, and why.
2. You will be more proactive in life, and in business, by coming from a position of awareness, strength, and strategy.

REVIEW provides the direction needed to plan your next steps so that you may make the changes necessary to **THRIVE, PROSPER,** and **SUCCEED!**

What can be pruned from your life? What beliefs, attitudes, choices, or regrets need to be lopped, cropped, and shed to set your energy free? The only way you will know is to take the time to **REVIEW** and discern what needs to be removed.

Note anything that has already come to mind. Your instincts are probably right.

"To thine own self be true."
—William Shakespeare

1. Reflect

"Self-reflection is a humbling process. It's essential to find out why you think, say, and do certain things . . . then better yourself."

—Sonia Teclai

Reflect . . .

1. **Think deeply or carefully about;**
2. **Contemplate, meditate, ponder, ruminate.**

Why Reflect? To better know your true self; desires; goals.

Moments of valuable personal reflection occur as you choose to spend time in calm deliberation and careful thought. Einstein was known for proclaiming that when he could not find the solution to a problem, he would lie down and take a nap. This is a habit that too few of us savor in our busy, competitive culture. We should take a lesson from Einstein, because he knew the importance of resting his mind and body. After doing so, when he woke, he would have the answer.

Imagine the thoughts and insights—and greater understanding of yourself—which could come to you if you would simply find the quiet space for them to be heard. To reflect is a welcome opportunity!

By intentionally reflecting upon any type of situation, you will gain clarity which you may not have achieved otherwise. It is during these quiet moments of expecting thoughts to flow and answers to surface that you can discover the right answers to your questions and calm any confusion you may feel in your life.

When I am feeling stress or overwhelm, chaos clutters my mind, blocking the flow of creativity and joy. If I choose to simply pause, breathe, and reflect, my world moves slower and at a more peaceful pace. It is in this calm reflection where I receive some of my best ideas and inspirations.

4 Ways to Make Reflection a Daily Habit:

1. Make the time, space, and place to capture a quiet moment and be still without distraction.
2. Candidly reflect upon your life—thoughts, feelings, ideas, experiences, and decisions.
3. Think, analyze, evaluate, and contemplate.
4. Let your imagination run free.

Taking time to reflect reveals solutions to problems, offers fresh ideas for innovation, and inspires your creativity. Reflecting on a daily basis will enrich your life by opening up new possibilities in your world.

"Your mind will answer most questions if you learn
to relax and wait for the answer."
—William S. Burroughs

2. *Reassess*

*"We live immersed in narrative, recounting and reassessing
the meaning of our past actions, anticipating the outcome
of our future projects, situating ourselves at the intersection
of several stories not yet completed."*
—Peter Brooks

Reassess . . .

1. **Assess again, especially while paying attention to new
    or different factors not previously considered.**

Why Reassess? Because almost nothing stays the same—you
have continuous opportunities for a fresh perspective.

Reflection from the last section has probably left you feeling
one of two ways—satisfied and feeling good about the things in
your life that came to light—or challenged and unhappy with
specific things that need your attention and determination to
change. If that's the case, please don't ignore it. Though that option
may feel preferable—your challenge, difficult situation, or need to
make a decision won't go away.

The person you are today is a result of the choices which
you've made, the influences of the people whom you've known, the
experiences that you've had, and the books you have read.

How's it all working for you? Are you pleased? If so, revel in the
joy that realization brings. Take a few minutes to feel grateful; few
things feel better than acknowledging what is working well and
feels right.

And if some things are not working so well, then starting right
now begin to reassess where you are and what you've done or

not done. Sometimes someone else's actions and choices forced you into this situation. It doesn't matter. Whether it was due to something you chose, or someone else chose, reassessing will open up variable options, as new facts come to light to help you make more informed choices moving forward. Whether your assessment encourages you to rest happily on your laurels or change directions, reassessment on a regular basis is valuable, whether it confirms or conveys it's time for a change.

My friend Russ once said to me, "You've never made a mistake in your life, because at the time when you made the decision, you thought it was your best choice at the time." Have you made a right decision in the past which would be a wrong one now?

Questions for Self-Assessment:

1. Are your *strengths* being utilized, personally and/or professionally?
2. Are you a *healthy communicator,* personally and/or professionally?
3. Do you maintain *high standards* for yourself, personally and/or professionally?
4. Are you proud of your *accomplishments,* personally and/or professionally?

Did you answer "No" to any of the questions above? If so, make a note about it, or them, here. Keep them in the forefront of your mind as the areas you want to begin to create change.

The upcoming chapters of "REVIEW" topics will help you know how to begin to produce clear solutions for the change you desire.

3. Reclaim

"To ignite your confidence and reclaim your courage, you must step into the highest vision of who you are. The only way to do this is to make the journey back into the arms of the Divine."

—Debbie Ford

Reclaim . . .

1. **Re-declare or take back ownership;**
2. **Make useful again; transform from a useless or uncultivated state;**
3. **Bring, lead, or force to abandon a wrong course of life or conduct and adopt a right one.**

Why Reclaim? To enjoy the return of something which was once yours.

Reflecting and reassessing may have left you realizing something important is missing in your life or that you have lost something you once placed a great deal of value upon. Do you yearn for its return? Would you like to get it back? Perhaps you can.

There was a time in my life when innocence and kindness brought emotional safety, trust, and stability. The world in which we find ourselves today, however, can be cruel, harsh, and daunting. To not be diminished by its negativity, I find that I must guard the door to my heart and head by reclaiming humor, optimism, and hope.

What Can You Reclaim? It Begins from Within . . .

- Reclaim your independence and self-reliance.
- Reclaim your confidence and self-esteem.
- Reclaim responsibility for your attitude, behavior, and choices.
- Reclaim your self-respect by standing up to bullies and not tolerating disrespect.
- Reclaim your seat at the table and your integrity by making your presence known.
- Reclaim your heart, sanity, and joy.
- Reclaim your time by being mindful of how you spend it.
- Reclaim your power by speaking up, standing out, and taking straightforward, honest action.
- Reclaim your positivity by surrounding yourself with happy and proactive people that want you to succeed.

4. Rethink

"Times of transition are strenuous, but I love them. They are an opportunity to purge, rethink priorities, and be intentional about new habits. We can make our new normal any way we want."

—Kristin Armstrong

Rethink . . .

1. **Change one's mind;**
2. **Think again about a previous decision;**
3. **Make a turn-around, flip-flop, or a reversal.**

Why Rethink? The first thought is not always the best thought; raise awareness that there is more than one right way to do things.

The progression of reclaiming things lost naturally causes you to rethink things in a different way. Possibility replaces pessimism because you are beginning to feel the personal power that is being released due to stepping up to face change or create change. Taking this seriously will assure you recognize and apply what you are learning on these pages. It's exciting!

Like most people, you have likely made decisions which appeared to be the right decision at the time, but once you reassessed your choice, you discovered it needed to be reversed or at the very least, amended. Rethinking gives you permission to use your thoughts to change your mind. If you need it, I'm giving you permission. It is okay.

When new information comes to light or new details are revealed, or your priorities have shifted, it is prudent to rethink your opinions and choices to stay in alignment with your values, stay relevant and stay informed and productive.

Rethinking takes what was previously known, or commonly accepted, and spins it around to give you a new review of the facts as you look at the realities of your life at this current time with a fresh perspective.

Whether rethinking confirms what you did right or illustrates the need to change direction, it is a valuable tool for your personal excellence.

One of my friends launched and grew a very successful business. She and her dedicated team had worked smart and hard to achieve their profitability, fine reputation, and community accolades. One day, she was approached by a large company who had admired their success. They proceeded to make her an offer she couldn't refuse. Her decision to sell or not to sell was not an easy one. She did not want to disrupt her employees or compromise the integrity of her vision.

She laid out different scenarios on paper, rethinking each idea for a while—flipping it up and down and all around, considering every pro, con, and angle along the way. Knowing that her final decision would have a lasting impact, she wanted to make sure she made the right choice for the best reason. Rethinking allowed her to move forward with confidence in selling her company with no regrets. Time has shown she made the right choice. My advice: sleep on it before you take a giant leap.

6 Steps to Rethink Something or Everything:

As you rethink something specific, which makes the most sense?

1. Disrupt
2. Shake-up
3. Challenge
4. Debate
5. Evolve
6. Transform

5. Reaffirm

"One of the processes of your life is to constantly break down that inferiority, to constantly reaffirm that I Am Somebody."

—Alvin Ailey

Reaffirm . . .

1. **State again as a fact;**
2. **Confirm the validity or correctness of something previously established;**
3. **Repeat your belief, saying, "This is so!"**

Why Reaffirm? It validates your opinions, decisions, and desired outcomes and it increases your confidence and conviction.

Affirmative words and actions confirm you are on the right path and help you attract what you desire. Whether you are reaffirming a dream, a goal, a previous commitment, or a person, reaffirmations identify and strengthen your possibilities. Begin reaffirming yourself and other people through encouragement, acknowledgments, a listening ear, and a spirit of gratefulness.

6 Things You Can Reaffirm

1. Reaffirm your employees to build emotional safety, their value, and a culture of encouragement in the workplace.
2. Reaffirm your customers to build relationships, repeat business, and their referrals.
3. Reaffirm to others that you can be trusted and depended on through words and actions. You do what you say.
4. Reaffirm your goals as needed to fortify your resolve.

5. Reaffirm your special talents and strengths to build confidence and healthy self-esteem.
6. Reaffirm your dedication to your mate, your family, and friends by demonstrating your love and loyalty.

Reaffirmations can disempower the critical voice that plays over in your head and creates self-doubt and worry. Shut that baby down and replace it with what *can be done* rather than what can't. And rather than allowing the judgmental opinions of others to bring you down, reaffirming will help you stay in tune, in touch, and on task with what you truly want and with what is good for you.

Positive Affirmations

Your thoughts have the power to change the function and structure of your brain. Repeating positive and specific statements can stimulate neuroplasticity, which enables you to retrain your brain by growing new neurons and connections. If you want to develop a mindset for success, first acknowledge which thoughts need to change and then replace them with ones that work in your favor. Since your thoughts become self-fulfilling prophecies, fill your mind with positive intentions and use positive affirmations to succeed.

How to Write Powerful Affirmations

- Ask yourself what you truly want.
- Write your affirmations, using, "I am," "I can," "I have," "I know," or "I do."
- Make statements positive and in present tense.
- Use passion, feeling, and emotion. Hope will prevail.

By reaffirming your desired outcomes as if they have already happened, you will activate the law of attraction and set the energy in motion to manifest whatever good you desire.

6. Remind

> *"People need to be reminded more often than*
> *they need to be instructed."*
>
> —Samuel Johnson

Remind . . .

1. **Prompt, cue, inform, retell.**

Why Remind? We are fallible human beings who can forget.

The overwhelming demands of daily living bombard us with continuous distractions, expectations, emotions, and responsibilities. We stay on the incessant treadmill—allowing others' need and demands to control us rather than realizing that we deserve to take control and live life in a way that works for *us.*

Is it any wonder that you have lost touch with simple pleasures? That life lessons you once knew and adhered to, that worked well for you, have long been forgotten? Seriously, considering the fast pace of life does it come as a surprise? I bet not.

Have you ever read a book or attended a seminar in which the content being shared served as a strong reminder of what you already knew? Perhaps some of the ideas were fresh and original, but the rest served as an excellent prompt to adopt it back into your life. We need those reminders every so often, in most all aspects of daily life.

Often when I am talking about an issue with a friend, she will remind me of something I already know. Her words will strike a familiar chord and help me get back on track to explore the issue with greater clarity.

A few times a year, I plan something outrageously fun and goofy simply to remind myself that life doesn't have to be so serious. How can you make play a part of your day to remind you of the joy found in living lightly?

8 Personal Reminders to Keep Your Life in Check

1. Always know you are valuable, important, and loved.
2. Determine to choose your attitude and create your reality.
3. Take control through your free will to make changes, and learn to say "no."
4. Choose to set boundaries; consider how you allow other people to make you feel.
5. Accept that failure and mistakes are an integral part of success.
6. Acknowledge that no one is perfect. It is okay to be imperfect and fallible.
7. Trust your best instincts and go with your gut.
8. Realize that everyone's life has a purpose and you are here for a reason.

Commit to memory the things above that stood out to you the most—and if you forget, this list is here to remind you! I encourage you to stay aware of these simple truths—be reminded.

7. $\mathcal{R}$etrace

"I claim to be a simple individual liable to err like any other fellow mortal. I own, however, that I have humility enough to confess my errors and to retrace my steps."

—Mahatma Gandhi

$\mathcal{R}$etrace . . .

1. **Go back over, repeat the same route, recap;**
2. **Discover and follow a route that worked successfully for another;**
3. **Trace something back to its original source.**

Why Retrace? When you look at where you have been, it will help you get where you're going.

If you are ever feeling lost or unsure of what to do, you can simply retrace the path that brought you to that particular place to begin with. Retracing will enlighten or remind you of what *to do* or what *not to do.* Have you ever misplaced something only to find it in short order when you "retraced your steps?" This same tool can be applied to your life experience.

Retracing Relationships

Have you ever reached a bad place in a previously healthy relationship and wondered how it had deteriorated to that point? Think about retracing your history with that person—back to a time when it was good, solid, and healthy—a time when you were happy and loved spending time together. Retracing may reveal clues from the past which are exactly what you need to help heal the hurt, forgive the past, and begin again.

On a humorous note, have you ever been so engaged in a conversation that you "run down rabbit holes," in diverse tangents? One of my friends calls it "tangisizing." My brother-in-law, Peter, from England, describes it as someone having "lost the plot." When this happens, retrace your conversation back to your original idea to help you get back to your intended point. It really helps!

As You Retrace, Truth is Evident

- Going back to the basics will remind you of what made you successful in the first place.
- History does repeat itself and will often provide clues or predictions about your future.
- Your past benchmarks can help you decide which direction to take next.
- When an important conversation takes the participants in different directions, you can retrace the points of discussion to return to the original intention.
- When you retrace your steps, you can more clearly see what was (and wasn't) done well. Either way, patterns will emerge, revealing if you should continue doing the same or to make changes.

8. Reevaluate

"Even if we have bad feelings about our past and it causes a sense of alienation, it belongs to our history. Its benchmarks are stored in the granary of our mind and crucial evaluations for the future cannot be made without consulting the archive of our memory."

—Erik Pevernagie

Reevaluate . . .

1. **Reexamine something in order to make changes, or form a new opinion.**

Why Reevaluate? It stimulates personal perspective and focus, and promotes the achievement of your goals.

It's extremely rewarding to retrace the path that resulted in a completed goal, since goals of all shapes and sizes are good. Even so, we know that it's one thing to set a goal, yet it's completely another when you get so caught up in the details that you neglect to review for viable and productive progress.

Periodic reevaluation is the key to increasing the chances of hitting your target. It's one way to improve and refocus. Doing this will better assure that you keep the initial goal in mind to avoid rabbit trails that take you off course. Or, alternatively, it is the key to changing the course of action if need be.

Staying Relevant

My website, www.SusanSpeaks.com, illustrates my brand, my services, my expertise, and my personality. Since I own my own company, I want to stay strategically positioned to ensure client engagement and motivation to the masses, offer free tools and resources, and touch as many lives as possible. To honor these objectives, it is imperative that I reevaluate my website on a regular basis. Whether it is to update the information, improve the graphics, empower the SEO, or add new content, reevaluation is an essential part of succeeding in my business.

Important Reasons to Reevaluate

- To ascertain if you are on the right track and heading in the right direction.
- To determine whether your hopeful outcome is within reason, is plausible, or is still worth pursuing.
- To substantiate the accuracy and viability of your plans, policies, and procedures.
- To tweak, improve, edit, or re-strategize.
- To discover what is and isn't working so that improvements can be made.
- To implement changes in real time to stay relevant and effective.

Hindsight is 20/20

"In hindsight, things are obvious that were not obvious from the outset; one is able to evaluate past choices more clearly than at the time of the choice."

—Wiktionary

History leaves clues and then repeats itself. Once you have completed a task or finished a longer project, reevaluation will help you know what you might do differently next time, or predict what may be coming in the future. There are clear patterns to follow—*or not!*

9. Readdress

"I don't have problems with people, because if I do, I address it."
—Wiz Khalifa

Readdress . . .

1. Look at or attend to an issue or problem again.

Why Readdress? It opens the door for healthy communication; to help, heal, clarify, and gain understanding.

If you have read from the beginning, you know that this book was born out of a conversation my adult children wanted to have with me regarding the events of their father's tragic and untimely death several years before. Not only did they want a better understanding, but they also needed to express how my communication skills, or lack thereof, had impacted them.

Since each of us processes life events differently, my viewpoint did not align with my children's perspectives of the life events and circumstances that we'd gone through together. At the time, for me as a mom, I wanted nothing more than to do whatever was necessary to ensure my children had as *normal* a life as possible. I have since learned that normal is an illusion; life is what you make it.

Through massive life changes, our family life was wrought with fear and heartbreak. As you can well imagine, I tried earnestly to be positive and create a happy home. But as parents, we gradually learn that we don't get to control all things. Like most mothers, I wanted desperately to protect my kids from pain and not burden them with my many worries. Unbeknownst to me, it had backfired, and years later they let me know it.

They shared that my "rose-tinted glasses" and persistent positivity had prevented us from talking about the hard stuff. As a result, it thwarted their communication skills for being vulnerable, authentic, and raw. It left too many things unsaid which would have helped us all heal faster and be healthier had we talked openly and shed the tears together. If I had known better, I would have done better. I know better now, and this can serve a purpose for you and your life, especially when faced with seemingly irreconcilable circumstances.

The Miracle of Readdressing

Opening this conversation has allowed each of the three of us a fresh opportunity to share our thoughts and feelings. Our love and loyalty for each other provided the emotional safety necessary to be vulnerable, authentic, and honest. Readdressing will serve to improve the quality of our communication for years to come, and will help us continue important healing. It is the exponential Power of Re^3!

My friend Cheri shares a secret sauce which she says can move mountains to heal relationships. It's worked for us, so I encourage you to try this. She says that to successfully readdress an issue, it takes these three intentional conversations:

- First, a person says what they need to say.
- Second, the other person gets the opportunity to listen and then respond.
- Third, both parties come together again to state their understanding, convey what they want to change, and reach an agreement on where to go from there.

How many conversations do you regret not having and wish you could go back to make right? Sadly, it's often too late!

This is a prime example. One of Cheri's clients wanted to be a professional fisherman. When he approached his father for financial support, his dad said, "No." He was devastated and wanted to give up. Cheri explained that that was only the first conversation and asked, "What might a second conversation sound like?"

In the second conversation, his father shared his belief that he should figure things out for himself and brainstorm on how to accomplish his goals on his own.

Finally, in the third conversation, the son finally spoke his truth. He told his father of the ways in which he had let him down, and how desperately he had always tried to get his validation and support. In this third conversation, he also said, "Dad, all I ever wanted was for you to be proud of me and support me."

An honest understanding grew between them, and shortly thereafter, his father was diagnosed with leukemia and died within three months. If they had not moved through these steps of readdressing, their discord would never have been resolved.

What crucial conversations need to be readdressed in your personal and professional relationships for you to gain peace, clarity, and resolution? Muster your courage, create the time and quiet space, and follow the steps above to begin to readdress what needs to be communicated and healed between you and another valued person in your life.

10. Reroute

"All human creativity mirrors GPS navigation."
—Mike Dooley

Reroute . . .

1. **Send someone or something by or along a different route.**

Why Reroute? It gives you new options when you have made a wrong turn, hit a dead-end, or have ended up in the wrong place.

I love the GPS technology in my cell phone and don't know how I ever lived without it. It has become a daily part of helping me get to where I want to be. Do you feel the same way?

One of the best features about the GPS technology is that when you enter your desired destination for where you want to end up, it will provide you with two or three routes from which to choose. In addition, if you make a wrong turn, your GPS will reroute your trip with new instructions to ensure you arrive where you want to go.

Very rarely in life will you go directly from point A to point B. You will undoubtedly encounter roadblocks, delays, detours, and potholes that disrupt or challenge your journey for achieving your goals. Don't get discouraged, that's simply the process of living life and moving towards your dreams.

Resolve to be flexible enough to make adjustments and to look for and find alternate paths to your desired outcome. Your attitude about the change of route will determine whether you perceive it as pain or gain. If you anticipate that the new direction will propel you into an interesting and beneficial adventure, you will stand in awe of the "reroute" experience.

11. Rewind

"Rewind your mental tapes and play them again. You may see and hear something new the second time around."
—Susan Young

Rewind . . .

1. **Return to an earlier time or stage in a sequence of events.**

Why Rewind? To re-experience a memory, a moment, or a feeling.

Do you remember seeing a TV show or a movie in which they would rewind the film and reverse the scene which had just occurred? Imagine a person taking a running leap into a swimming pool and splashing everyone sitting nearby.

Now rewind the scene in your mind, with their actions reversed and the water going back into the pool so that everyone is dry again. While you may not be able to rewind things physically, going back and looking at events mentally may allow you to notice aspects which you might not have seen before.

This visual illustrates the value of rewinding scenarios in your own life, relationships, or behavior, to help you pay attention to things that you may have missed the first time around.

Play It Again, Sam

There are times when I cannot sleep at night. As a nocturnal exercise, I will rewind my mind to the good times when I lived in my family home, in my first apartment, in our various dream homes, where my babies were born—and move chronologically through the years.

At each home, I take a mental walk around, and then move onto the next one. As I immerse myself in the sights, sounds, colors, and fragrances, I am reminded of many experiences of love, a secure home, and much happiness and comfort. Considering I have lived in over sixteen places, the memories are rich and rewarding—and quite a long walk! Ultimately, this practice helps me fall asleep.

Just as you might rewind music to enjoy the lyrics over and over again, rewinding your good memories and appreciated moments replays the movies of your life. I hope you enjoy the show.

4 Scenarios to Rewind (but not at bedtime)

1. Rewind a conversation to the beginning and replay to identify how misunderstanding may have occurred and to learn how to better convey your message to aid in understanding next time.
2. Rewind a decision which ended up having unanticipated consequences in order to influence future decisions.
3. Rewind heartbreak in order to face, accept, and heal old wounds.
4. Rewind a careless word or criticism and replace it with a compliment or kind word.

> *"The big advantage of a book is that it is very easy to rewind.*
> *Close it and you are right back at the beginning."*
> —Jerry Seinfeld

12. Resolve

"The difficulties you meet will resolve themselves as you advance. Proceed, and light will dawn, and shine with increasing clearness on your path."

—Jim Rohn

Resolve . . .

1. **Settle or find a solution to a problem, dispute, or contentious matter;**
2. **Decide firmly on a course of action.**

Why Resolve? To find answers to questions and solutions to problems, to reach mutual agreement, or to tie up unfinished business.

Have you noticed that many companies are now calling their sales reps and customer service teams "Solution Specialists?" They have wisely learned that people want their problems and issues resolved.

Think of the word "resolve" as a re-solution. You take a current situation that is not ideal to discover new solutions that help you achieve what is ideal. So, whether it is through your products, services, or consultative methods, being a problem solver builds loyalty and confidence among your customers, your team, and those you work with.

What would you like to resolve? Are there questions for which you are seeking answers? Do you have a challenge that seems impossible or unsolvable? With the root word being "solve," resolve is one of your best strategies for clearing the path, overcoming obstacles, and achieving solutions.

I approach my business in the same way. To ensure that my clients receive strategic solutions from our time together, I will perform a "needs assessment" by asking discovery questions. From these, I learn what challenges my clients are facing, what gaps exist, and what goals they want to achieve in a particular timeline. It is my mission to help them resolve their problems so they can accomplish their objectives. I follow up through my keynote presentations or custom designed training to give them the tools to make it happen! *Problem re-solved!*

8 Ways to Resolve Problems

1. Create the time and space for thought and contemplation.
2. Call a trusted friend for advice, guidance, or ideas.
3. Search for reliable solutions on the Internet.
4. Go to YouTube to learn how to do it.
5. Read books for pleasure and for fresh perspective and education.
6. Speak to an expert who has the answers.
7. Join a mastermind group for synergy and feedback.
8. Hire a coach for guidance, support, and accountability.

"Don't dwell on what went wrong. Instead, focus on what to do next. Spend your energies on moving forward toward finding the answer."
—Denis Waitley

13. Regroup

"There are times in life you just have to cut your losses, regroup, and move on with your life, and never look back."

—Nishan Panwar

Regroup . . .

1. **Settle or find a solution to a change, challenge, problem, or dispute.**

Why Regroup? As you step back for a moment to look at the big picture, you will see the *how, where,* and *what* of the roles you are playing so that you can make changes where needed and reorganize to get back in the game.

After a 15-year working relationship, Cheri's office administrator left to pursue a new opportunity. While at first her departure was a shock and an unwelcomed change, it became a powerful catalyst to see how the team could rise up, become innovative, and positively bounce back. After tearful good-byes and reluctant acceptance, Cheri rallied her team to discover where they would go from there.

With fresh eyes, her team came together to regroup to say, "This is where we are and what our team looks like now. It's a big loss, but what are we going to do moving forward?" They found creative, strategic, and positive ways to make their culture better than ever. Regrouping is a critical part of adapting to change—it is a series of proactive measures that acknowledge the change, adjust for recovery, and then begin to re-position you for success.

5 Ways to Successfully Regroup

1. Slow down to go fast. Stop, contemplate, and reflect before making any further changes.
2. Be honest and transparent. Question everything.
3. Don't make huge changes all at once, but be willing to observe and reconsider; have the tough conversations, as individual roles shift or have further demands.
4. Seek outside help from a coach, consultant, counselor, or advisor to mediate, stimulate, and help implement needed solutions.
5. Gain buy-in from the people who will be impacted to unify for a shared mission.

Drop Back and Punt

Football provides an excellent metaphor for regrouping. When a team is in possession of the ball, but cannot advance its agenda any further, they must "drop back and punt." Doing this requires that they step back to reassess and reorganize their strategy in pursuit of winning the game. When your prospects are looking dim and your options are limited, "drop back and punt" to approach your activities from a renewed vantage point.

When you are faced with change and apply this regrouping process, you are better equipped to make decisions. Think new opportunity as you take each new step. Rather than settling back into old habits and doing what you've always done, create something fresh, original, and awesome.

"Growth is a spiral process, doubling back on itself,
reassessing and regrouping."
—Julia Margaret Cameron

14. Reappraise

"When one cannot appraise out of one's own experience, the temptation to blunder is minimized, but even when one can, appraisal seems chiefly useful as appraisal of the appraiser."

—Marianne Moore

Reappraise . . .

1. **Appraise something again or in a different way to discover its current value.**

Why Reappraise? As values change, reappraisal keeps you informed, enlightened, and aware of something's worth.

For sixteen years, I enjoyed a prosperous real estate career. Regardless of what price my sellers may have purchased their homes for originally, the current marketplace determined their home's value when it came time to sell. As conditions change, new appraisals are needed.

Using this analogy in your own life, ask yourself what needs to be reappraised to determine its current value.

- Are there things which you valued greatly in the past which are now worthless to you? Acknowledge them without regret or guilt and adjust your activities and energy to align with what you now value.
- Are the people around you adding value or diminishing it? Consider loosening or tightening your boundaries with them accordingly.
- Is your career de-valuing your talents and efforts by not utilizing your strengths? Recognize the worth of the

strengths you possess and consider these if you seek a career change.

- Are you investing in yourself to improve your sense of value and self-worth? Investing in self-enrichment and improvement is an insurance of sorts; it will empower and protect you in case of sudden change or calamity.

The sudden changes I shared in the beginning of this book made me feel like the Queen of Calamity. As our real estate values plummeted and investment accounts evaporated, the fear was so great it made me physically ill. I was too ashamed and embarrassed to reach out for help and kept my suffering a secret.

I felt like I was treading water and could not find a solid bottom upon which to stand. Once the storm finally passed, it took incredible courage to assess the collateral damage and accept this unfamiliar reality. It required reappraising the values in my life so that I would know what resources were available to help me rise again. By thoughtfully reappraising aspects of your life, you too will gain insight for what holds value and truly matters.

"Rock bottom became the solid foundation upon which I rebuilt my life."

—JK Rowling

15. Reinterpret

*"Reality is how we interpret it. Imagination and volition play
a part in that interpretation. Which means that all reality
is to some extent a fiction."*

—Yann Martel

Reinterpret . . .

1. **Interpret something again in a new or different way;**
2. **Examine the meaning of something again and find a new and different understanding;**
3. **Explain from a different point of view.**

Why Reinterpret? Your first impression, assumption, or understanding could be incorrect, skewed, or in need of more information to see the big picture or the real truth.

Each person is one-of-a-kind, with a unique view of life that is influenced by and dependent upon his or her upbringing, personality, and   personal experiences in this world. Your perception is totally your own—it is an individual interpretation of life, events, circumstances, lessons, and people. Changing your perception will alter your interpretations and therefore, your reality. One of my favorite philosophies for understanding the differences among people and their attitudes is *There is no reality. There is only perception.*

Many a message from another has been misconstrued or lost in translation because it was not interpreted correctly. One of our greatest communication challenges is to fail to see another person's perspective.

If you feel like you're hitting a wall because you simply don't understand something, or another person has a different approach, keep your mind open. Be willing to reinterpret it with fresh eyes, more information, a change in position, or a new perspective.

This old adage may prompt you to reinterpret someone's words, actions, or feelings: *Walk a mile in my shoes, see what I see, hear what I hear, feel what I feel, then maybe you'll understand.*

16. Respond

"How you respond to the challenge in the second half will determine what you become after the game, whether you are a winner or a loser."
—Lou Holtz

Respond . . .

1.   **React, answer, reply, react favorably.**

Why Respond? It allows you to engage with others in a calm, healthy, and appropriate manner for a productive, respectful, and proactive conversation.

Emotional Intelligence

EI (Emotional Intelligence) means: the capacity to be aware of, control and express one's emotions, and to handle interpersonal relationships judiciously and with empathy.

The ability to respond with dignity, discretion, and wisdom is a mark of a person's character and EI (Emotional Intelligence). The first two steps to improving your EQ (Emotional Quotient) are developing greater self-awareness and enhancing your capacity for self-regulation. When each is developed and improved, a person is more likely to respond thoughtfully than to react carelessly.

Breakthrough versus Breakdown

When change happens, you have a choice in how you are going to respond. You can either lose your composure and react impetuously or use the event or situation as a learning opportunity to shift your mindset and respond appropriately. Begin to notice your responses when changes occur:

- Do you react with resistance and uncontrolled emotion?
- Do you anger easily and regret actions later?
- Do you hold onto bitterness, grudges, and resentment by complaining?

OR . . .

- Do you accept the change and adjust accordingly?
- Do you look for gifts in the pain and learn the lesson?
- Do you realize that to adapt to the change, YOU may have to change?

Regardless of your answers to these questions, become aware of whether your initial responses are typically helpful or hurtful to yourself or others. *You might not be able to control the changes around you, but you can certainly determine how you choose to respond.* It's your choice. Be smart about it.

The Energy Leadership Index

ELI (Energy Leadership Index) is an attitudinal assessment which will help you evaluate how you respond to change in situations by measuring your energy and action. Your attitudes, behaviors, and abilities in a crisis reveal your character, personality, and coping skills. Be willing to use the information about how you respond as a way to gauge your personal growth without judgment or condemnation. Use this assessment to become more aware of the ways that you're being triggered or feeling you're a victim. Learn to use your responses in this exercise as a guide for responding well in the future.

The Dreaded Drama Triangle

Many of us react to change from a victim mentality without even realizing it. Respected psychiatrist Steven Karpman designed the "Drama Triangle" to illustrate the roles we play when we are caught in drama. The three roles are: The Persecutor, The Rescuer, and the Victim. Which, if any, of the three roles—Persecutor, Rescuer, Victim—rings true for you?

Regardless of which one we are playing, the triangle can be a hotbed for denial, guilt, shame, anger, fear, dishonesty, blame, and pain. People who are operating from a victim mentality will often respond in one of four ways:

1. Fight
2. Flight
3. Freeze
4. Appease

To become the creator of your life and stand in your power, choose to remove yourself from the "Drama Triangle." The great news is that shifts happen and you can learn to respond and participate in a more favorable way. Rather than staying stuck in drama, you can enjoy empowerment and more favorable outcomes by:

- Being a Creator rather than a Victim
- Being a Coach rather than a Rescuer
- Being a Challenger rather than a Persecutor

To explore more and implement Steven Karpman's game-changing solutions, check out his book, *The Power of TED: the Empowerment Dynamic*.

17. Remember

"Keep your dreams alive. Understand to achieve anything requires faith and belief in yourself, vision, hard work, determination, and dedication. Remember all things are possible for those who believe."

—Gail Devers

Remember . . .

1. **Recall knowledge from memory, have a recollection;**
2. **Recapture the past, indulge in memories;**
3. **Keep in mind for attention or consideration.**

Why Remember? It brings forward wisdom, thoughts, feelings, and details which will reliably guide you in your current life changes and choices.

Can you remember? Sure you can. Think of a time when you felt happy, competent, healthy, powerful, successful, capable, vibrant, energetic, strong, confident, or serene. If none of these adjectives describes you, come up with ones that do! Now, step back into your memory, and remember what it felt like when you inwardly felt that way and outwardly put it into action. Breathe in the memory of that time in your life, feel it, and recreate it. What you once felt can come forward and be felt again.

If you are ever in a place where change has disrupted your flow or shifted your once solid foundation, you can use your memories to re-ground you. As if brick-by-brick, bring these positive emotions and previous actions forward. Remembering and reliving your memories will influence your mind and change your current state—and begin to get you unstuck.

Many writers, me included, will experience writer's block which shuts down our flow of inspiring ideas and creativity. While attending the Hay House Writer's Conference in Chicago, Nancy Levin, author of *Jump and Your Life Will Appear,* guided us through a powerful writing prompt. The exercise helped us get unstuck, and get back to writing with enthusiasm and energy.

Nancy asked all of us to pull out a piece of paper and at the top, simply write, "I remember . . ." She then gave us five minutes to write as fast as we could about a significant memory in our past. We were to fill as many pages as possible in that limited timeframe. The exercise was transformational for me and the others. This personally creative exercise spurred our memories to remind us that our own life's experience is a rich and wondrous resource for remembering possibility and probability for our life.

Remember that you are a unique creation designed for a sole purpose; you bring as much value as any other person on earth.

When and if you're feeling fear, remember a time when you were courageous and brave. When you're feeling sad, remember a time of laughter and joy. If you ever feel lonely and unloved, remember a time when you were embraced and fulfilled by loved ones. These memories can help you transition through a change with gratitude and strength.

8 Benefits of Remembering

1. Remembering people's names makes them feel important.
2. Remembering happy times will comfort you during life's challenges, changes, or difficulties.
3. Remembering important dates tells others that they are special and bring value to your life.

4. Remembering mistakes from the past will help prevent you from repeating them.
5. Remembering your blessings will make you more grateful.
6. Remembering your truest self will serve to make you more authentic, humble, compassionate, and kind.
7. Remembering your successes will fortify you when you stumble.
8. Remembering to listen will make you a better communicator.

"We do not remember days, we remember moments."
—Cesare Pavese

18. Requalify

"At the heart of personality is the need to feel a sense of being lovable without having to qualify for that acceptance."
—Paul Tournier

Requalify . . .

1. **To be right for—to measure up;**
2. **Change something slightly, to limit or add conditions to.**

Why Requalify? If you have ever been denied, rejected, or lost your ranking—step up, step out, and keep trying until you qualify, ultimately achieving your goal.

You change. People change. Circumstances change. Finances change. Employment changes. Relationships change. And at each step, the qualifications to participate may too.

An interesting thing about one's qualifications is that they shift and change on a continuously evolving scale. Just because you did not qualify for something in the past does not mean you will not qualify now. Just because you do not qualify for something now does not mean you will not qualify for it in the future.

The NBA superstar Michael Jordan did not originally qualify for his high school basketball team; however, he never gave up and kept on trying. Because of his tenacity, he not only requalified himself, he went on to win six national NBA championships and changed sports history.

If you truly want to qualify for something, discover what needs to be fixed, changed, or resolved to make it possible. One of the best examples of re-qualifying I've seen is in mortgage applications. I remember having clients who couldn't qualify financially to buy a home. However, once they consolidated debt, sold a car, or paid off a student loan, they would qualify for their dream home.

Whether it's an athlete trying out for a sports team, a hopeful student being accepted into a Master's program, a political candidate qualifying for office, or a newlywed couple buying their first home, life comes with qualifications.

We have all heard stories about authors who submitted hundreds of query letters and book proposals which were continually rejected. Yet because of their persistence and refusal to give up, they finally got published and became best-selling authors.

When we don't qualify for some reason, it may be the perfect opportunity to step back, look at our goal and ask, "Do I really want it?" If you're dedicated to making it happen, the only way you can fail is to stop trying. Be creative. Be constructive. Never give up if it is something you deeply, passionately, enthusiastically desire.

"The ability to qualify for, receive, and act on personal revelation is the single most important skill that can be acquired in this life."
—Julie B. Beck

19. Requantify

"The trick is to realize that counting, measuring, and tracking is not about the result. It's about the system, not the goal. Measure from a place of curiosity. Measure to discover, to find out, to understand. Measure from a place of self-awareness. Measure to get to know yourself better. Measure to see if you are showing up. Measure to see if you're actually spending time on the things that are important to you."

—James Clear

Requantify . . .

1. **Recount or express something in numbers, re-measure, re-specify, re-determine.**

Why Requantify? It allows you to measure things numerically to provide a sense of certainty, objectivity, and credibility.

Quantifying, calculating, weighing, and measuring are happening in your life all the time. A recent Facebook funny I read online said, *Well, another day has passed and I haven't used algebra once.* Isn't that the truth? Even though using algebra may not be one of your normal activities, math plays a vital role in how you live in this world.

6 Requantifying Questions:

1. How are things adding up, personally and professionally?
2. What needs to be literally (and figuratively) subtracted from your life to relieve stress and promote a healthy well-being?
3. Can you divide the work with others to get more done and be more efficient?
4. Would you like to multiply your social life and make more friends?

5. What percentage of your time is spent doing things that really matter? Create a pie chart to get a clear picture.
6. Have you weighed the risks of your decision? Do your answers of "yes" outweigh your "no's?"

Quantities are all around you and these brief examples are a lighthearted illustration that show how quantifying and requantifying is an excellent practice to measure various aspects of your life.

What Can You Requantify?

- Measure the progress you are making on your hopes, dreams, goals, and strategies.
- Track your schedule, activities, and due dates for project management, accountability, and completion.
- Measure sales calls against closing ratios.
- Count your caloric intake to track your diet.
- Establish the ROI (Return on Investment) before making an investment or purchase.
- Calculate mileage and distance to estimate the time of arrival while travelling.
- Improve your GPA to earn a college scholarship.
- Create a budget to monitor your income and expenditures.

Many analytical people do not believe that a goal is worthy unless it is measurable. They want quantifiable facts and figures to show how their bottom line is being impacted. It helps them see whether they're making progress or lagging behind. If you are numbers-minded, this comes naturally to you. If you're not, consider quantifying your activities as a great way to track your progress.

20. Reconsider

"Inspiration is not garnered from the litanies of what may befall us; it resides in humanity's willingness to restore, redress, reform, rebuild, recover, re-imagine, and reconsider."

—Paul Hawken

Reconsider . . .

1. **Consider something again, especially for a possible change of decision regarding it.**

Why Reconsider? By keeping your mind open, you may discover a sense of flexibility and confidence, adventure and awe that takes you to places you may never have imagined.

Reconsideration creates a great opportunity for you to contemplate a previous decision, opinion, action, behavior, or position. "Second-guessing" can at times be very helpful. Have you ever felt strongly about something, but when you considered new information which came to light, you changed your position? Of course you have. We all have.

In the crafts of sewing and construction, the expression "measure twice, cut once" is a wise axiom to ensure a greater chance of success. Taking a measurement more than once usually results in greater accuracy and correct action. This is especially critical if the outcome is irreversible. Look before you leap and you will have fewer regrets.

Maintaining an open mind, as you reconsider with an open heart, exposes you to unlimited possibilities—and will set the stage for extraordinary experiences and outcomes. Reconsider your options to welcome and enjoy new adventures, expand your territory, and transform your current reality.

Reconsider the Possibilities

When my children left home, I still felt an obligation and responsibility to maintain a family home so they would always have a place to come home to. Although my man, my sweetheart, lived a thousand miles away, and we were tormented by our separation, I decided to stay in Florida to be available for my children and loved ones. After months of loneliness, I reconsidered my options. By acknowledging that everyone has their own journey, and facing that I needed to start living mine, I reconsidered moving to Wisconsin.

Although it was a very difficult decision at the time, it has proven to have been the right one. I have grown exponentially in the two years I have lived here, and achieved things which may never have happened. I am truly grateful to have reconsidered the possibilities.

Just because something has not yet been done, does not mean that it can't be done. Just because something did not work in the past, does not mean it cannot work in the future. Just because you have failed in your attempts, so far, does not mean that you will be denied wild success in the future. Reconsider your options and possibilities.

6 Things Worth Reconsidering

1. Reconsider asking for help when you need it.
2. Reconsider being vulnerable and authentic.
3. Reconsider how much money you're saving.
4. Reconsider if you are happy with your life.
5. Reconsider changing careers for advancement.
6. Reconsider simplifying life, to calm the chaos.

Which of these "strike a chord?" List the first things that come to mind which you can reconsider for change.

21. *Reawaken*

"Some people awaken spiritually without ever coming into contact with any meditation technique or any spiritual teaching. They may awaken simply because they can't stand the suffering anymore."

—Eckhart Tolle

Reawaken . . .

1.   **Awaken once again, arouse, wake-up;**
2.   **Emerge from physical, spiritual, or emotional slumber.**

Why Reawaken? Moving toward an enlightened and informed mindset encourages a shift in consciousness which taps into your intuitive nature and timeless knowing for truth.

Time is passing lightning fast and you are burning earth years. Your moments in this lifetime are fleeting, so use the time you have now and ahead to utilize your amazing skills and gifts to the fullest—and leave your mark. And in the words of Brendan Burchard, *Live, Love, Matter!*

Every morning you get to awaken to a new day. And every night as you sleep, you will hopefully experience rest, renewal, and rejuvenation.

The zombie apocalypse television shows have been wildly popular and have created a cult-like following. Sadly, we see many people who live their lives that way. They are unengaged, uninvolved, non-committal, and blowing in the wind.

While it is evident they are breathing, walking, and talking, they seem to be asleep at the wheel, wandering aimlessly, *without any plan* or a desire to wake up and live the life of their intentional making. Their lives are spent missing the possibilities and staying stuck in unhappy lives.

In real life, some people choose to exist in that state, while others would love nothing more than to live a joyful and productive existence. The problem? They do not know how to awaken, get unstuck, and get moving.

These simple wake-up calls will keep you from slumbering during the times you would rather not!

Wake Up! Your Life Is Calling!

7 Concepts to REWAKEN to:

1. You have unlimited choices and possibilities from which to choose.
2. You can embrace and act on new opportunities.
3. You are surrounded by beauty.
4. You can be restored and inspired by the sights, sounds, and smells of nature.
5. Gratitude for your freedom and blessings expands your abundance.
6. You have the ability to find and create solutions.
7. You can love your life.

Your Ego versus Your Essence

In the striving, stress, and struggle of our daily lives, it is easy to lose sight of who we truly are. The ego is so busy handling our affairs for survival, it often overrides the calm essence at our core.

Your *essence* is your eternal and ethereal source for love, harmony, acceptance, wisdom. It is an unlimited connection to a higher source and purpose. Everything in life becomes more profound when you are a co-creator with Spirit.

The ego is your logical and rational mind. It can guide you well in your thinking and pragmatic approach. However, it can also create emotional responses which spur on judgment, intolerance, fear, worry, and hate. Wayne Dyer defined ego as, *Edging God Out.* Which one guides your life more often—your ego or your essence?

My friend Cheri's own life-coach, Daniela Popa, encouraged her to speak this affirmative daily mantra to help guide her in living a happy and fulfilling life: "Today, no matter what I'm doing, no matter who I'm doing it with, and no matter where I'm going, it is my dominant intent to please myself because it brings me joy and puts me in alignment with my spirit. That is the greatest gift I can give the world."

Isn't there a place of pure joy where we would all love to live? When you focus on connecting with your truest essence, that spiritual center of love and acceptance, you will reawaken to aspects of yourself you cannot yet imagine.

2nd Power
Redo

Redo

Now that you have reviewed what is working, realized what's not, and have gained understanding about what needs to change, you will begin to see everything from a new perspective. In this new light, you will discover ways to prune, shift, shed, shine, fix, change, or improve, to create something better than you've known before.

Do you hold fond memories in your heart which you would like to experience again? Have you made mistakes which you wish you could go back and correct? Has life turned out differently than you had planned or wanted?

Have changes been imposed upon you which you did not want or desire? Are you unsure of your next steps? Are you ready to be proactive in making positive changes to create more positive experiences? The wonderful thing about second chances is that you get to take what has already happened—and REDO it!

Why *Redo*?

1. You may find more happiness, success, energy, connection, tranquility, and joy.
2. You may discover "new and improved" ways of evolving, and new processes for surviving, striving, and thriving.
3. You can take pieces of what used to be, put them together again and create a preferred new result.

"Sometimes you have to kind of die inside to rise from your own ashes and believe in yourself and love yourself to become a new person."

—Gerard Way

22. Refocus

"Every new day, we must refocus, to see the beauty of the moment."
—Lailah Gifty Akita, *Think Great: Be Great!*

Refocus . . .

1. **Focus attention or resources on something new or different;**
2. **Put again into focus or focus more sharply.**

Why Refocus? Getting clear and concise will help you create a single-minded priority for the thing(s) you truly want to accomplish.

Please take note of this: *Whatever you focus on will expand, so be very mindful of where you are focusing your energies and how you are focusing your thoughts.* Changing your focus is one of the most important steps you can take for shifting your mindset to attract the outcomes you desire.

In the words of Tony Robbins, *"Where focus goes energy flows."* If everything feels like a grind or a challenge, take a moment and ask yourself, "What has my focus been on?"

If you focus on the negatives about yourself, about others, or about situations and problems, they will continue to persist. When you focus on the *positives and solutions,* however, it's as if invisible hands come from the universe to help you along your journey with the solutions.

When you dedicate focused thought, focused strategy, focused energy, and focused effort to any situation, your singleness of purpose will work as a catalyst to help you achieve your goals.

If you truly want to create new and positive change, stop

focusing on the old stories, or the negative reruns that persist in your mind.If you're trying to change your life to become the new improved version of your former self, refocus on what you want, so that you can break free from what you once were and what you are determined to leave behind.

Visual Victories

My brain is easily distracted by the next big idea or new shiny object. Squirrel!

Through the years, I have experimented with many focus-building methods, and have finally discovered what works best for me. I have adapted as needed to fit my personality style. As a visual person, I need big, bold, visual lists to keep me on task and give me a sense of accomplishment.

Whether I am planning my marketing strategy for my business, handling project management for my writing projects and books, or dreaming of home projects, I use a dry erase board with colored markers. I have three boards in different rooms in my house so there is always one nearby to capture my *brilliant ideas* as they arise, or make a note of a task which needs to be done. There is also an intrinsic satisfaction which comes from drawing a line through the items I have completed. What a sweet reward! What methods work best for you?

10 Ways to Tame Your Monkey Brain

1. Minimize distractions.
2. Clear the clutter from your desk, your home, and your life.
3. Write everything down to provide you with visual tracking.
4. Finish first things first and don't buy into the myth of multi-tasking.

5. Prioritize your most important tasks.
6. Set up habits and systems to help you get and stay organized.
7. Delegate the little stuff that slows you down, or is not in your wheelhouse.
8. Enjoy the process and find pleasure in your activities.
9. Work in sprints, not marathons, to maximize short bursts, rather than get burned out by the long haul.
10. Get centered, grounded, and laser focused.

The Power of Focus

Here, there, everywhere! In our fast-paced and distracted society, we are constantly bombarded by short news cycles, information overload, and interruptions. Our 'short attention span epidemic' has forever changed how people read, learn, and process information. Generations have not only adapted to the short staccato pace of Facebook and Twitter, but it is now the "new norm." In our hectic lifestyles, 'focus' has become a rare and valuable commodity.

Developing your power of focus, however, is one of the most important things you can do for living a productive life. Bestselling author and pastor Rick Warren shares, "There's awesome power in a focused life. Diffused light doesn't have much of an effect on what it touches. But when you focus light—like the sun's light through a magnifying glass—you can light a piece of paper or grass on fire. If you can focus it even more, it becomes a laser. A laser can cut through steel and destroy cancer." Imagine the magic that can happen when you simply FOCUS!

Focus One Course of action Until Successful

23. *Reframe*

"Successful transformations reframe the problem and that makes the solution possible. They erase existing boundaries and start from scratch."
—Malcolm Gladwell

Reframe . . .

1. **Frame or express (words, a concept or plan) differently;**
2. **Change the conceptual and/or emotional setting or viewpoint.**

Why Reframe? By considering the same information in a different context you can get a completely new perspective on it, enhancing your understanding.

We're all familiar with the "spin," that is achieved through providing a biased interpretation of an event to persuade public opinion. Similarly, your "frame of reference" will color your world. It is based on your beliefs, opinions, experiences, proximity, interpretation, and more. The frame we put around a person, place, thought, or idea, defines the meaning which we give it. As soon as we change the "frame," the meaning for us can also change.

Reframing encourages independent thinking, as you say, "I want to look at this another way." By changing the frame around a situation, you not only change your perception of it, but its meaning to you.

If you were to take one painting and try it in three different frames, each combination would offer a completely different impression and presentation. Your frame of perception works the same way.

Simple Words

"Would you please reframe that and change your wording into something I can better understand?" How many times have you needed to ask this of people who were talking "over your head?" We've all had this happen with folks who are so highly educated in their area of expertise, they don't realize that we mere mortals do not understand their medical/technical/scientific terms and jargon. When this happens, we need to ask them to reframe their information, and put it in laymen's terms. This helps to make even the most complex concepts simple and understandable.

How Can You Reframe Things?

- Ask another person's opinion. Maybe two people's.
- Change your space, place, or location to see the situation from a different angle. Evaluate as if you were responding from an entirely different demographic.
- Reformulate or reinterpret what other people are saying. This might require stating back to them what they said.
- Rephrase the words you use in your sentences to enhance their meaning. Always consider your "audience."
- Try to remove emotion from the situation and then reframe it with facts and logic. Take a more objective approach.

24. Reinvest

"Invest in bettering yourself and the future you. Let your future self-look back on the changes you make today and be thankful you made them."
—Marianne Williamson

Reinvest . . .

1. **Re-empower, give qualities or abilities to something or someone;**
2. **Dedicate resources for potential growth or profit.**

Why Reinvest? Capitalize, rearrange, augment, and improve upon investments you have already made to realize an even better return.

You have tremendous resources and assets simply by virtue of breathing, being safe and able, and being alive. In addition to these birthrights, you are hopefully blessed with time, energy, loved ones, friendships, health, money, intelligence, and untapped resources.

Have you invested your time, effort, energy, heart, money, and soul in places that are performing poorly, dragging you down, causing pain, or are a losing proposition? Perhaps its time to move it all elsewhere to achieve richer rewards and better returns.

Earning a great return on your financial investments requires reinvesting wisely. The concept of reinvesting applies to more than money. It also applies to the intangible assets from which you can reap the greatest return. Are you reinvesting in what matters most?

Reinvesting Creates New Opportunities for You to . . .

- Build upon or enhance what is already working well.
- Improve your efficiency, effectiveness, and productivity.
- Put your resources into areas that matter most to you.
- Be proactive to achieve the results you desire.
- Connect with your passion, purpose, and progress

During the time that our country was in economic turmoil and upheaval, my personal financial assets and investments felt like they were on "Mr. Toad's Wild Ride"—paralleling my life situation at the time. Some areas performed well, while others tanked. Perhaps this happened to you as well. If it didn't, I am sure you know many people who were impacted. It brought fear, indecision, confusion, and a dread over not knowing which next steps would be the most prudent. Restoring balance after the storm required me to reinvest, rearrange, restrategize, and reconsider my options, if I were to enjoy financial serenity and stability once again.

6 Important Reinvestments

1. Reinvest in your personal growth, in the ways most meaningful to you.
2. Reinvest in your relationships with love, attention, time, nurturing, and healthy, heartfelt connection.
3. Reinvest your time in priorities that matter—*to you.*
4. Reinvest in your state of mind through managing stress, by reawakening to the hopeful and positive.
5. Reinvest in your body with regular exercise and sound nutrition.
6. Reinvest in life experiences and meaningful moments to create happy memories, through deliberate planning.

25. Reassign

"When a man begins to do that which is assigned to him,
it becomes as if he is more endowed and favored than his fellows."
—Ogwo David Emenike

Reassign . . .

1. **Attribute, allocate, designate, or re-dedicate for a special purpose;**
2. **Move someone or something to a new location or position.**

Why Reassign? Because there may be a better space, place, or purpose—a better way or an enhanced meaning for the situations in our lives.

Reassignment of Meaning

"Being human always points, and is directed, to something or someone, other than oneself—be it a meaning to fulfill or another human being to encounter. The more one forgets himself—by giving himself to a cause to serve or another person to love—the more human he is."
—Viktor Frankl

So much of our suffering grows out of the emotional attachments we assign to an experience, regret, or a judgment. Drop the judgment and the need to reassign its meaning and you can free yourself from its pain. Could the struggle and strife we experience be caused by self-created illusions that result from our interpretations and limiting beliefs? Perhaps yes.

Consider the optimist versus the pessimist who have the same experience, but the different meaning each assigns results in completely different outcomes. If you have a struggle in your life which is keeping you in pain or regret, reassign its meaning by first looking at it objectively without any emotion to see if the facts support the fiction. Release the judgment for a moment, by remaining detached and neutral. Enjoy the freedom that comes from this moment of relief.

In his book, *Man's Search for Meaning,* the prominent Jewish neurologist and psychiatrist Viktor Frankl describes the horrors of being imprisoned in a Nazi concentration camp during World War II, where both parents and his pregnant wife perished. He witnessed how those who assigned meaning to even the most horrific of circumstances were more resilient and fortified to maintain hope for survival.

Frankl wrote, "Everything can be taken from a man but one thing, the last of the human freedoms—to choose one's attitude in any given set of circumstances, to choose one's own way." He continues to say, "This uniqueness and singleness which distinguishes each individual and gives a meaning to his existence has a bearing on creative work as much as it does on human love . . . He knows the "why" for his existence, and will be able to bear almost any "how."

Reassignment of People

Leaders understand the importance of assigning the right people to the right tasks to get the job done well. This is most crucial when they are not fulfilling their obligations.

In his book, *The Energy Bus,* Jon Gordan shares how fundamental it is to put the right people in the right seats. If you put the wrong person in the wrong place, no matter how talented they are, they will never reach the peak of their potential. Not only will their strengths be underutilized, but it will be a continuous struggle for them to measure up to expectations. Most of us, at one time or another, have had jobs that we were not well-suited for, or worse.

I once knew a lady who was bright, eager, and determined to work for one of my client organizations. Each time I would go to train the various teams, she would be in a new and different group. I asked her why, and she shared that she had been moved several times to ensure she would be the right fit for the job, the team, and their mission. After being reassigned over three times, she finally found the place where her talents and strengths could best serve.

Are you willing to trust the process enough to reassign the positions for which you lack interest?

When my friend Cheri reviewed her volunteer commitments, she realized there were multiple positions in her life which she did not enjoy. By giving up her seat and reassigning her position, she made room for someone who was more passionate. Perfect!

What Can You Reassign?

- Delegate a task to someone who, due to a skill set, can do it better than you, in a more timely fashion, or at a lower cost.
- Share the workload with others to get it done faster and more efficiently—oftentimes this improves team effort and effectiveness. A win-win.
- Reassign an employee to a different department if there are personality conflicts.
- Reassign the meaning you are giving to a situation, a person, an assumptions, or an outcome.

26. Rebrand

"Rebrand is not just about buzzing brand words; it's about repurposing your lives, finding your true voice and building an authentic brand that impacts lives. It's a call to reexamine our lives, our goals and dreams; to think about why we do what we do, to align lives back to source (God) and connect with the hearts of people. It's a movement, to help, to add value, to create meaning, to impact lives."

—Bernard Kelvin Clive

Rebrand . . .

1. **Change the image of a person, corporation, or organization.**

Why Rebrand? Our changing world often requires us to change right along with it so that we stay fresh, relevant, and engaged.

It Might be Time to Rebrand When . . .

1. Your brand, once relevant and effective, becomes worn out or outdated. (Companies know that to successfully grow their market share and maintain their competitive edge, it is imperative for them to rebrand for a positive top-of-the-mind consumer awareness.) On that note, take a step back and decide which areas of your life could also use rebranding.
2. You have grown above and beyond your original skills set, experience, and vision—and need to develop and introduce the latest, new and improved you.
3. You have new offers, products, services, and solutions, and need to reintroduce yourself and your updated and refreshed business positioning to the public.

4. You want to seize new opportunities by tapping into and attracting a new target market in which you display who you are, what you do, why you do it, and where.

Rebrand for Personal Transformation

Rebranding doesn't only apply to business. It is the proverbial facelift. I have known many friends who were ready for a massive life overhaul. Their priority? Transform every area of their life to achieve greater happiness and well-being.

Cheri, my friend that I've referred to throughout these pages, got to a point where she simply wanted to feel better and be healthier. She never wanted to diet again, but wanted to *release poundage.* (Notice I did not say 'lose weight' because that would indicate that it would return.) Rather than excercising self-sabotage and critical condemnation, she changed the way she loved herself. She began to celebrate her body, fill it with life-giving nutrition, and move and groove, as she enjoyed heart pumping energy shifting endorphins. She chose to remove all sugar, whites, and caffeine from her diet, and to run three times a week.

Her weight fell off so fast her clothes no longer fit. We went shopping for an entirely new wardrobe to celebrate her new body, life, and brand. With her credit card and my personal eye for color and style, we went shopping and she got a new attitude and an entirely new experience.

She looks and feels amazing. People hardly recognize her, and are stunned by her new awesomeness. She reflected on and wanted to reclaim what was lost. Through personal resolve, she chose to rebrand—and an upbeat attitude accompanied her as she transformed from the inside out. Beautiful!

What Can Be Rebranded in Your Life?

- Your attitude (anything that needs to take on a fresh image)
- Your vision, values, and mission statement
- Your personal style—haircut, wardrobe, jewelry
- Your business, including your website, logo, graphics, business card, social media, marketing, and promotion

By giving your old brand a fresh new twist you will not only illustrate your desire to stay relevant, it might even help you to be perceived and received in a more positive light.

27. *Realign*

"Don't reinvent the wheel, just realign it."
—Anthony J. D'Angelo

Realign . . .

1. Align anew or better, line-up, adjust.

Why Realign? When we are out of alignment, it wears down our parts, pieces, energy, resolve, and essence, resulting in undesired consequences.

When the wheels of your car are out of alignment, not only are the tires and other parts worn down and damaged, but steering and the quality of the ride are adversely impacted. Likewise, when your spine is out of alignment, you may experience pain, headaches, and poor posture, all resulting in a diminished quality of life.

Alignment works the same for every other aspect of your life. You know what it feels like when you are out of alignment physically, spiritually, emotionally, or mentally. It wears you down, stresses you out, and negatively impacts your health and well-being. When you're out of alignment, life is more of a struggle, tasks become harder, and relationships may encounter more conflict. How does it happen?

Realigning Our Relationships

When a relationship gets out of whack, it can create untold suffering, misunderstanding, mistakes, heartache, and emotional shutdown. If an important relationship is feeling fragile, make the effort to realign and put it back on track. Whether you are realigning your values, your expectations, your roles, or responsibilities, your efforts to realign will demonstrate your level of commitment and loyalty. It will inevitably strengthen your overall potential for a healthy outcome with that person—also repairing what was broken or had gone wrong.

Cheri had a trustee whom she felt was her nemesis. He would fight, resist, and criticize her every step of the way. She scheduled a time to meet with him, by requesting time for an honest conversation about what was happening between them, since they were going to have to keep working together.

After authentic and mutually respectful communication, they reached an agreement about certain things they both could agree upon. It changed all of their dealings and interactions moving forward. Realignment allowed them to get on the same side of the issues. Walking parallel, they no longer crisscrossed the other, and became an integral part of the solution, not the problem.

Identify Causes for Misalignment

- What is causing stress and conflict?
- What is draining your energy?
- What is making you feel bad?
- What symptoms is your body exhibiting?
- Do your thoughts match your actions?
- Are you holding onto grudges and resentments?
- Are you living in alignment with your integrity and values?

Feeling unsettled? Align your integrity with your actions. Reaffirm your intention. Once you realize what may be causing misalignment, make a concerted effort to close the gaps, realign, and feel true to yourself, effective and dynamic again. Readdress and reinterpret as needed.

28. *Recapture*

"Any intelligent fool can invent further complications, but it takes a genius to retain, or recapture, simplicity."

—E.F. Schumacher

Recapture . . .

1. **The act of taking something back;**
2. **Capture again, retake, or experience anew.**

Why Recapture? When you are stuck in a rut and no longer experiencing happiness and fun, you can return to your natural joy and playfulness.

Years ago, when going through a very difficult time in my marriage, I went to a family counselor for guidance. With tearful sadness, I told him I was a naturally joyful person, but I had lost it. I asked, "How can I recapture my joy?"

He wisely shared, "Susan, your joy has never left you. It's been buried beneath sensory blockages. Remove the sensory blockages, and you may find it again."

His truth gave me hope that my joy could return. And it did. For you, what has gotten buried beneath life's rubble that you want to recapture? It will take a little rearranging and a little time, but as you change how you "do life," (by simply putting each word below into daily thoughts and actions) you will recapture the joy-filled things you long for. You can choose to say YES to the prizes of life, especially valued intangibles such as these.

Be reminded—you are engineered for health, vitality, and resilience, yet years wrought with challenge and difficult circumstances can rob you of life's greatest free gifts.

8 Essential Prizes to Recapture

1. Fun
2. Hope
3. Health
4. Yourself
5. Laughter
6. Creativity
7. Spontaneity
8. Dreams

Make it a habit to choose one of these "prizes" each day. Do what is possible to integrate "it" into your daily activities. Add to this list any other boon of the good life you wish to recapture.

Rethink: What has shut you down? What do you want now? What were your dreams? Restore them to your life and recapture the treasured things which bring you joy.

"The world is larger and more beautiful than my little struggle."
—Ravi Zacharias

29. *Reprioritize*

"Time management is an oxymoron. Time is beyond our control, and the clock keeps ticking regardless of how we lead our lives. Priority management is the answer to maximizing the time we have."

—John C. Maxwell

Reprioritize . . .

1. **Reorder in rank of importance;**
2. **Reassign a rank or rating to.**

Why Reprioritize? As life happens and changes occur, things in our lives shift in their order of importance.

When something is a priority, it takes precedence over other things because of its importance or sense of urgency. When your priorities are not well-ordered, you may experience incredible stress and discord—letting yourself and others down. This takes its toll on those prizes of the good life that you recaptured in the last chapter.

Look again at 20. Reconsider again, and all that is currently happening to you, and you might discover that you need to get your priorities straight! Priorities which once took precedence may need to be rearranged and shifted around simply because of changes or demands in your life.

We've all got the same bucket of twenty-four hours in a day. A powerful indicator which differentiates those people who succeed from those who fail is how they choose to prioritize their time.

As a young woman, I took to heart the story about the college professor who stood in front of his classroom with a clear bucket. As he placed big rocks, pebbles, and sand (in that order) in the bucket, he would ask, "Is it full yet?" And each time his students would say, "Yes!" At last he poured in water which truly filled it to capacity. The lesson of this exercise is that if you fill your life up with less important activities, you might not have enough time (energy, money, etc.) left over to take care of the things that truly matter.

Your life and schedule work the same way. If you spend all your time taking care of things that don't help you, make you money, serve your higher good, or that drain your energy, you're simply not going to get the most important stuff done.

Learn to prioritize—*in fact, to reprioritize.* Do first things first! When you put your daily priorities in proper order, you will get more done and enjoy a sense of completion and accomplishment. You deserve this feel-good gift you give yourself—a 'prize' to add to your list from the last chapter!

9 Steps to Reprioritize Your Day and Get More Done

1. Envision everything you want or need to get accomplished.
2. Itemize your to-do list.
3. Rank each task in its order of importance, by grading it as an A, B, or C.
4. Create a new list with the A's, B's, and C's in order of importance and urgency.
5. Since your A's are of utmost importance and priority, plan your activities, dedicating your complete focus to them first.
6. Focus on one thing at a time and do not multi-task.
7. Minimize distractions and do not allow them to undermine your results.
8. Ask for help if needed, and delegate where possible.
9. As you accomplish each item, cross it off. Your mini victories will reward your efforts and help you build momentum.

"To-Do Lists" are essential if you want to enjoy peak performance and personal transformation. When you *DO NOT* use them effectively, you will experience more stress and be less focused, less organized and less productive. When you *DO* use them effectively, you will feel more empowered, efficient, focused, and successful.

Now, with all of that said, there is another process for reprioritizing which is critical for you to live a balanced, happy, and healthy life. It's about taking a bird's eye view and looking at the bigger picture.

What really matters to you in life and is most important right now? Is it your family? Your career? Your health? Your hobbies and leisure? Your money? Be forewarned that if the less important things use you up, the most important things may suffer from neglect. And be reminded, too, that reprioritizing happens frequently, depending on the ebb and flow of life. While you answer the questions below, ask yourself, "What makes me happy?

Ask yourself:

1. What are your most desired goals?
2. Where do you find your greatest joy?
3. What priorities matter the most in your life?
4. Whom do you enjoy spending the most time with?
5. What activities would you most like to experience?
6. What gives you a sense of accomplishment and fulfillment?

My friend Jason Kotecki is a best-selling author and highly sought after speaker. His marketing materials confirm: "Life balance is a top priority for Jason. With a young family, he only accepts a maximum of 52 invitations to speak each year. That being said, his schedule fills up fast, so don't hesitate to contact us to learn more about bringing him to speak to your organization."

There is no doubt here that Jason has intentionally ordered his priorities. His family and quality of life are more important than anything else.

When you continually reprioritize your life by knowing what brings you the most joy and fulfillment, life is rewarding beyond measure. Getting your priorities in order will truly help you achieve this.

Your Absolute Yes List

Bestselling author and speaker Cheryl Richardson has inspired me for decades with her practical and inspirational wisdom for living life well. In her book, *Life Makeovers*, Cheryl writes, "Creating an Absolute Yes List will help you to remember your priorities, especially when your life gets hectic and you feel like you're losing time. Having this list handy makes it easier to focus your time on the things that are most important, and in doing so, to identify the things that are a waste of time. After all, once you're clear about the yeses, the nos become easier to define too." Begin creating your Absolute Yes List to help you reprioritize your time, your life, and your relationships.

> *"The key is not to prioritize what's on your schedule, but to schedule your priorities."*
> —Stephen Covey

30. *Retrain*

"Amateurs train until they get it right, professionals train until they can't get it wrong."

—Unknown

Retrain . . .

1. **Redevelop, reeducate, re-prepare.**

Why Retrain? Continuously honing and refining your skills and awareness gives you the competitive edge for success and fulfillment.

Considering that I am a professional speaker and trainer, this is a fun chapter for me to write. If people did not need ongoing growth, development, motivation, and education, my career would dissolve. However, people worldwide are in continuous need of personal and professional enlightenment and direction to live their best lives.

Whether you are seeking to achieve peace and harmony, learn a new technology to do your work faster, or design a strategy to blow your competitors out of the water, retraining is a pivotal way to strengthen your knowledge and realize your goals.

What Can You Retrain?

- Retrain yourself to remember that which has been forgotten.
- Retrain yourself to improve your skills, talents, and performance.
- Retrain your team to empower synergy, unity, and collaboration.

- Retrain your sales people to improve their closing ratios.
- Retrain your office on new policies, processes, products, and services.
- Retrain your muscles to make you stronger and improve your health.
- Retrain your family to put their dishes straight into the dishwasher.

7 Advantages of Retraining

1. It expands your knowledge and awareness.
2. It teaches or reinforces skills, concepts, tools, and talents.
3. It can shift your mindset and confidence; help you thrive.
4. It can make you more efficient, effective, and productive.
5. It stimulates discussion and enriches education.
6. It keeps your mind sharp and continuously evolving.
7. It encourages open-mindedness to learn something new which you didn't know before.

When children are learning how to walk, we don't criticize them when they fall down. We encourage them to get back up and try again. Separate yourself from judgment and condemnation. Instead, give yourself permission to be a beginner again—*and feel okay to begin again.* If at first you fall, get back up and keep trying.

"There isn't anything that isn't made easier through constant familiarity and training. Through training we can change; we can transform ourselves."

—Dalai Lama

31. *Redesign*

"If you don't design your own life plan, chances are you'll fall into someone else's plan. And guess what they have planned for you? Not much."

—Jim Rohn

Redesign . . .

1. **Design anew, make a new design.**

Why Redesign? Continuously honing and refining your skills and awareness gives you the competitive edge for success and fulfillment.

Research and development teams use redesign as a success strategy to ensure they work out the kinks, get the job done right, and build value. When a prototype is designed, it is tested, retested, refined, and redesigned as many times as necessary it to achieve its best result.

Did you once have a grand plan that felt so right, but now you find it no longer serves you? If there are areas in your life which simply need to change to help you create better results, a redesign may be in order. This realization brings with it new learning. . Revising the original blueprint, in your head or on paper, can create new possibilities for better results. The smallest modification can result in plan perfect!

6 Reasons Why a Redesign May Be Necessary

1. To evolve into something more than before: the original design needs to be edited, developed, corrected, or improved.

2. To learn from mistakes: The original design was an utter and complete failure and you need to start over from scratch.

3. To improve your purpose: You have achieved the goals you set out to achieve and now it's time to move to the next level.

4. To broaden your goals: Your environment has changed and no longer fits your needs or supports your objectives.

5. To face facts: Your needs may have changed, and you have outgrown your situation or your situation has outgrown you.

6. To become more flexible: Your management style has to adapt and integrate with the changes in your culture.

What Needs to be Redesigned in Your Life?

- Your goals.
- Your life game plan.
- Your daily habits.
- Your order of priorities.
- Your career plan.
- Your financial goals.
- Your diet and nutrition.
- Your relationships and social life.
- Your living space.
- Your own growth and development.
- Your fun, leisure, and hobbies.
- Your schedule and use of time.

Imagine that you want to redesign your backyard. Even if you don't have the resources for redesigning it, picture yourself renting a bobcat to remove all of the dysfunctional and unwanted plants and weeds. Clean the landscape; create a blank canvas upon which to start a brand-new design that grows literally from the ground up.

A crucial part of redesign is being willing to demolish what doesn't work. Cleaning the slate to start anew is a reckoning of sorts.

From there, allow yourself to imagine what the new design will look like. Realize that it may take only one small redesign to positively impact everything else. Nothing stands still.

Life by Design

After a 30-year career with the US Air Force (with her last fifty-three months being stationed three-hundred miles away from her husband and two sons), my lifelong friend Chief Dina Moriarty returned "home" to begin living her happily ever after.

Having risen to the ranks of the top one percent of the Enlisted Force, her transition was hard. She had gone from leading thirteen full-time Chiefs, two-hundred Reserve Chiefs, and more than thirty-five-hundred Airmen to being home full-time. She felt displaced and disenfranchised. Both boys were moving on in their lives, and her husband had settled into his own routines. She didn't fit in.

She soon realized that to find purpose and stay sane, she had to redesign her life. Using her meticulous skills as a military member, wife, and mom, she became a Professional Life Organizer. She began helping people organize their lives, homes, tasks, and even their businesses. She found great joy in using her talents to help others become more empowered, organized, and efficient. After eighteen months, she closed the business and began organizing people's lives on a voluntary basis. Five years and five grandchildren later she continues to redesign her life by trying new things, learning new talents, and serving others. A redesign is always in order!

32. Rebuild

*"When defeat comes, accept it as a signal that your plans
are not sound, rebuild those plans, and set sail once
more toward your coveted goal."*
—Napoleon Hill

Rebuild . . .

1. **Reconstruct, dismantle and reassemble with new
   parts;**
2. **Replace, strengthen, reshape, or reinforce.**

Why Rebuild? Once something has been destroyed or damaged beyond repair, it must be rebuilt or replaced if you are to thrive and enjoy normalcy again.

When Hurricane Katrina hit the Gulf Coast in 2006 it left devastation in its wake. To deal with the destruction left by the storm, entire cities, towns, and communities had to rebuild. They had no other options if they were going to thrive again.

Have you ever experienced such a shattering season in your own personal life? A time when death, divorce, financial loss, failure, or disaster changed your world to such an extent that you weren't sure how you could ever rebuild again?

Being determined to clear the debris from the aftermath is a courageous and necessary first step. It strengthens your resolve and enables you to build exactly what you need, fulfilling your greatest hope and desire. Where can you begin?

Which of These Do You Hope to Rebuild?

- **Life**—after it has fallen apart.
- **Confidence**—when you have failed.
- **Team spirit**—when a toxic manager leaves.
- **Self-reliance**—when you have been dependent.
- **Reputation**—after poor choices and indiscretion.
- **Stamina**—to be persistent and go the extra mile.
- **Self-esteem**—that has been trampled, used, and abused.
- **Financial security**—after unemployment, credit debt, or bankruptcy.
- **Relationships**—that need to heal from neglect, misunderstanding, or heart break.

Rebuilding takes tremendous effort and energy. What you rebuild has to be something in which you are invested to begin with or it will not be a worthwhile endeavor.

6 Must-Haves to Rebuild Anything

1. A vision
2. A blueprint
3. Materials and resources
4. Tools
5. Time and commitment
6. Helpers

"Don't be afraid to start over. It's a new chance to rebuild what you want."
—Anonymous

33. Repair

"If it can't be reduced, reused, repaired, rebuilt, refurbished, refinished, resold, recycled or composted, then it should be restricted, redesigned or removed from production."

—Pete Seeger

Repair . . .

1. **Fix or mend something; restore to good working order.**

Why Repair? Something valuable is worth saving.

Some people come from the mindset that "if it ain't broke, don't fix it." Life proves that sometimes things need to be broken, then repaired to make them right again.

In our throw-away society, valuable things are too often trashed. Similarly, people can feel loss of value, and literally discarded. The good news is that repair, within us, is always possible.

What Might Need to be Repaired within You?

- Broken trust or a broken heart
- Tarnished reputation or status
- Damage done by an incompetent leader
- Damage done from a toxic person or traumatic event

You Have to Care to Repair

If you have a car in need of repair which you don't particularly care about, then you'd be happy to trade it in for a new one. But if it is a car you love, you might spend whatever it takes to get it fixed and running well. People will "put good money after bad" if it is for something they really care about. The same applies to relationships—and more importantly, your relationship with yourself.

Measure the personal value to determine whether you invest, emotionally or financially, in repairs. When you truly treasure and respect something or someone, repairs are worth the investment of your time, energy, heart, and resources.

Repairing Relationships

If you or anyone you care about has ever been through a divorce, you know how challenging it can be. The brokenness is often poignant, painful, and excruciating. After my own divorce, my ex-husband grew hateful and mean. Thankfully, as time went on, our relationship improved and finally evolved into one of mutual acceptance.

For the love of our children and respect for our shared history, we began to repair our relationship the best we knew how. It improved so much that he and my new man Daniel became good friends and spoke often.

Two months before he died of a massive heart attack, he joined us for his last Thanksgiving dinner. As we shared in the holiday festivities, there was a lightness and joy that healed our hearts and helped us understand that repairing relationships is more than possible. It can be miraculous.

34. Readapt

*"It is not the most intellectual of the species that survives;
it is not the strongest that survives; but the species that survives
is the one that is able best to adapt and adjust to the changing
environment in which it finds itself."*

—Leon C. Megginson

Readapt . . .

1. **Adapt anew, re-modify fittingly;**
2. **Readjust oneself to different conditions, environment, circumstances, etc.**

Why Readapt? Your ability to be resilient in times of change will empower you to thrive in the most challenging of circumstances.

Change is going to happen regardless of whether you want it to or not. Expecting it gives you a heads-up and a head start. Your ability to adapt to it right away will determine your level of resilience. Every time there is a change which creates a new and unexpected reality for your life, you go through a three-step process: *orientation* (comfort zone); *disorientation* (confusion); *reorientation* (a new reality).

The speed at which you move from disorientation to reorientation will be determined by your ability to readapt—to find your feet on solid ground and step forward, no matter the weather. When you can do this in a healthy and thoughtful way, you will inevitably be more resilient.

As a lifetime Floridian, I grew up with perpetual summer and warm temperatures. At the age of fifty-one, I moved a thousand miles north to be with my wonderful man, Daniel, in Wisconsin. Talk about a change of environment! I had to trade my flip-flops for

Wisconsin Badger boots!

Readapting to the climate, the harsh winters, and the differences in the culture has been a perpetual adventure to say the least. It's been one of my more challenging personal changes, due to being so far away from my close family and friends. This has required me to readapt, appreciating them and their visits all the more. Precious.

As we hike through and discover new territory, the beauty of change emerges all around us. An example in nature is chameleons. They naturally adapt to change, while still being true to themselves. When they find themselves in a new environment, they will change their colors to fit in. This also keeps them safe and helps them to survive and thrive.

Like the chameleon, you may also find yourself in a new and changing environment. How can you change yourself to integrate and succeed? This is not change to the point that you become inauthentic, but rather, you become more situationally aware, increasingly intuitive, and considerate of the people around you. Learning to be a social chameleon will enable you to navigate situations with ease and adapt to your circumstances.

Resisting change and failing to adapt can compromise your position in experiencing a satisfying life, diminish your effectiveness in an organization, create relationship struggles, and lead to missed opportunities. Learn methods for readapting so that you too may find the confidence, safety, and ability to thrive in most any environment—in your personal and business life.

10 Ways to Readapt in Times of Change

1. Shift your mindset and attitude; *refocus* to have a healthier relationship with change.

2. Be proactive and take responsibility for how you respond.
3. Find gifts in the pain and seek lessons which may be learned.
4. Shed limiting belief systems.
5. Change your expectations.
6. Be brave enough to stretch beyond your comfort zone.
7. Ask for help when you need it.
8. Focus on what you want more of.
9. Stop blaming, naming, judging, and making excuses.
10. Forgive yourself and others.

"I'm such a chameleon. I never get bored!"

—Natalie Imbruglia

35. *Recover*

"Recovery involves a process of growth and transformation as a person moves beyond an acute distress and develops new-found strengths and new ways of being."
—Mental Health Commission of Canada, 2010

Recover . . .

1. **Return to a normal state of health, mind, or strength;**
2. **Rally, recuperate, regain vigor.**

Why Recover? It allows your body to heal, repair, and replenish your energy to return to a state of health and vitality.

How many times do you say these things to others? "Get well," "Hope you'll pull through," or "I know you'll make progress." How about saying these same words of encouragement to yourself?

While recovery is normally associated with regaining health after an illness, an addiction, or an injury, it applies to an unlimited number of scenarios and experiences which can set you back, keep you stuck, and cause suffering in your life.

Recovery is the affirmative outcome you'll enjoy once you have moved through a setback and arrived successfully on the other side. The sooner you find ways to achieve solutions for recovery, the faster you will regain vitality, hope, and well-being.

Conditions from Which to Recover

- Burnout
- Mistakes
- Betrayal

- Infidelity
- Shame
- Assault
- Addiction
- Heartbreak
- Bankruptcy
- Depression
- Health Issues
- Embarrassment
- Devastating loss
- Rejection
- Being fired or laid off
- Relationship discord

5 Ways to Begin Recovery

1. Create the time, space, and place for allowing you to recover; rest, breathe, reflect, and forgive.
2. Acknowledge what you are feeling; avoid denial.
3. Focus on the positives; what is, not what isn't.
4. Be introspective about what could have been different, what you control, and *can do* to begin to recover.
   Surround yourself with uplifting people, see a therapist or counseling professional, or visit a support group.
5. Take actions which will strengthen, bolster, empower, and support you in your recovery.

You lead a very busy and productive life, or most likely you wouldn't be reading this book. I would bet that you often burn the candle at both ends. The first step, when you feel depleted, is to make time for recovery or you will not able to continue at a normal pace. Take an occasional sick day from work and nurture mind, body and soul—to recover your ability to give 100 percent plus on the job!

Self-nurture by lying on the couch in your pajamas all day—sleep, eat, watch TV, read—and simply rest. Give yourself permission to slow down and recover. Begin identifying other ways that you can self-nurture and recover, regardless of what life throws at you.

For some people, it's taking a walk in nature. For others, it is eating healthy and exercising. What are some other things that you can do to recover and feel your best? When you are feeling unhappy, stressed, or imbalanced, make your recovery a priority.

"We live in a world that celebrates work and activity, ignores renewal and recovery, and fails to recognize that both are necessary for sustained high performance."

—Jim Loehr

36. Redirect

"Sometimes the slightest things change the directions of our lives, the merest breath of a circumstance, a random moment that connects like a meteorite striking the earth. Lives have swiveled and changed direction on the strength of a chance remark."

—Bryce Courtenay

Redirect . . .

1. **Channel into a new direction;**
2. **Cause to go somewhere else.**

Why Redirect? When you find yourself going in the wrong direction, stop, look, listen; use all the tools available to you to find the right way to your preferred destination.

The great thing about redirecting is that if you miss the mark and miss your goal, you can simply change course. When you are heading down a certain path, but you're not sure if you're going the right way, use a compass or stop and ask for directions—and sometimes, you might even choose to take another path. In time, the reason for the altered course will make itself known to you.

What Can You Redirect?

- Your focus
- Your energy
- Your priorities
- Your physiology
- Your conversation

Don't focus on what *you don't want,* because that is exactly the direction you will be heading if you do. Instead, ask yourself what you *do want* and direct your attention and energy towards it.

Over Steering

Have you ever driven a boat? If so, you have found that changing your direction on the water can require great foresight and effort before the boat fully responds. Sometimes you have to over-steer to shift position. Once the boat begins to turn, however, you steer in the counter direction to get back on a straight course. When you change directions in your life, be aware that too much redirecting might take you too far, and somewhere that you had not intentionally planned to go.

Your life story needs your proactive attention—to evenly steer and *redirect* "character, setting, and plot" as is needed. In doing so, your life will have a consistent theme and stay on course.

Don't Let Your Wake Drive the Boat

Speaking of boats, water, and staying on course, Dr. Wayne Dyer shared a brilliant metaphor for releasing your past to move in the direction of your dreams. Imagine you are on a boat and the horizon ahead represents your future. As you are steering the boat, your present-moment energy is moving you forward. Behind you, you will see a turbulent and frothy wake which has left a trail of foam. It represents the past.

Are you living in the present and choosing a deliberate course of action, or do you continuously look back and allow the events of your past to preoccupy and dominate your thoughts? Begin to redirect your attention to the present moment so that your focus drives you to where you want to go.

37. Rebalance

"Be aware of wonder. Live a balanced life—learn some and think some and draw and paint and sing and dance and play and work every day some."
—Robert Fulghum

Rebalance . . .

1. **Restore equilibrium or return balance;**
2. **Rearrangement of priority or weight to achieve evenness, equality, proportion, or stability;**
3. **Harmonious arrangement or relation of parts or elements within a whole.**

Why Rebalance? Nurture and meet the needs of each and every essential area in your life life and you will live in poise, stability, and well- being.

Successfully juggling the demands in your personal and professional life may feel like a daunting and unrealistic task. Employers know all too well that if an employee's personal life is suffering, their work life will too. And vice versa. Even the most self-aware and diligent person can be challenged. How can you balance your life to prevent burnout and promote well-being?

10 Ways to Bring Balance Back

1. Become self-aware and take an honest inventory of where the imbalances are occurring.
2. Stop, breathe, and be mindful; live in the moment.
3. Find your fun and relearn how to play and tinker.
4. Schedule dedicated downtime to relax, reflect, regroup, recharge, and renew.

5. Minimize contact with dream stompers, spirit suckers, energy busters, or those who live in continual high drama.
6. Be selective of your priorities and choices that contribute to whole health living.
7. Exercise for energy, strength, stamina, and mental clarity.
8. Spend quality time with loved ones.
9. Volunteer to be in service to others who are less fortunate.
10. Savor your blessings with humility and gratitude.

Areas of Imbalance

- **Time**—do you have more things to do than you have time to do them?
- **Diet**—do you moderate your intake with food and drink that replenishes your body or depletes it?
- **Priorities**—are the most important things in your life taking a back seat to things that matter less?
- **Reciprocity**—are you giving back as much as you are receiving?
- **Hormones**—when hormones are out of balance, it impacts your health on all fronts. Does anything need attention for improved health?
- **Self-talk**—is it more negative than positive? Is it full of self-doubt and self-recrimination? Are you overthinking?
- **Wanting vs. Having**—happiness is not only about having what you want, but wanting what you have. Try to live in acceptance and appreciation for "what is," not moping about "what isn't."

The Wheel of Life

Your well-being is a system comprised of many parts. When one part, or area, gets more attention than another, imbalance to the whole results. Smooth out the bumpy road by finding the balance needed to enjoy calming comfort and fulfillment.

- Health
- Family
- Spirituality
- Relationships
- Intimate Partner
- Emotions
- Home
- Career
- Finances
- Educational/Learning
- Fun and Enjoyment
- Social Contribution

"Life is like riding a bicycle. To keep your balance,
you must keep moving."
— Albert Einstein

38. Revise

"I've found that in business, opportunities will constantly emerge or situations develop that make you revise your plans along the way."

—Benjamin Cohen

Revise . . .

1. **Alter or improve a preliminary draft;**
2. **After reviewing again, make adjustments, edit, or amend.**

Why Revise? Life is a living document which requires editing and revision as our stories unfold.

It is Wise to Revise

Revision means "re-vision" and gives us an opportunity to look at the big picture to see where adjustments need to be made. It is an essential activity for people who work with the written word. Whether it be policies, procedures, instructions, articles, books, laws, contracts, amendments, or sales proposals—revising enables us to edit for improvement and elaboration.

Even with an email, it is wise to read it two or three times before sending. Your revision ensures that your message is being clearly communicated so that the receiver thoroughly understands your tone and intent.

Texts, sent quickly, can have typos and be dangerously sketchy when self-correcting technology changes your words and distorts your intentions. Don't presume with an email, text, or in life, that the final draft is as you wish if you haven't taken the time to revise as you go.

Revise as changes occur and new information becomes available. Be willing to take the time to go back, look again, and consider where and how you can make adjustments in order to stay in alignment with your vision, mission, passion, and purpose.

A Living Document

In our work and in life, we can and should lose the fear of being wrong, or having to shift gears in the middle of the road. For example, just when I thought I had this book's content and beautiful graphics all wrapped up nice and tidy, it was evident that it was still being developed. I reconsidered what it would take to make it even better.

Walking my talk, I decided to "Review, Redo and Renew" the entire *Release the Power of Re³* book. It was a great reminder that life, and everything in it, is a living, breathing, ever-changing document. Nothing is set in stone, never to change. As a writer, I knew that revision could transform my working draft and it did.

Move beyond revising only the written word, and consider the ways in which you can revise your life. You are a human working draft and can seek ways to revise your life story. Welcome the opportunity—learn to love and allow ongoing revision—all it takes is an attitude to adapt and a willingness to do so.

Rather than rehashing the past, know that your life is alive—active and vigorous . . . vital and spirited—and can be changed at any time to demonstrate those priorities and so much more!

"It's never too late – in fiction or in life – to revise."
—Nancy Thayer

39. *Refuse*

"The first step toward success is taken when you refuse to be a captive of the environment in which you first find yourself."
—Mark Caine

Refuse ...

1. **Decline, deny, resist, reject, pass up, turn down, spurn, or show unwillingness.**

Why Refuse? There are times when saying "yes" is simply not in your best interest.

In the pursuit of trying to be all things to all people, or trying to live up to another person's expectations, do you ever find yourself saying "Yes" when you wish you had said "No?"

Have you ever found yourself in a situation that called for you to lose your integrity, betray your values, or made you feel pressured to agree? Times like these require that you simply learn to say no for self-respect and preservation.

Saying "no" to things which do not matter or lack priority in your life is a valuable strategy for self-preservation. When you rightly refuse, it prevents you from being stretched too thin, overwhelmed, over-committed, and obligated to responsibilities which do not bring any benefit to you or your family.

Ironically, saying "no" can also help you help another person by not enabling them to become co-dependent. It's often said, "You should not try to do for another what only she or he can do for herself/himself."

Ask yourself: *When have I agreed to do something I really didn't want to do because I was more concerned about the other person's feelings or circumstances, even at the risk of damaging my own?*

"Refuse" is not a Bad Word

"There comes a time in your life when you walk away from all the drama and people who create it. You surround yourself with people who make you laugh. Forget the bad, and focus on the good. Love the people who treat you right, pray for the one who don't. Life is too short to be anything but happy."

—Jose N. Harris

There is freedom and power in having the courage to refuse. For years, I have heard that once a person reaches the age of fifty, most of their decisions will either be a "Hell yeah!" or a "Hell no!"

When I hit my fifth decade, I found this to be true. I am now more able to clearly see the big picture clearly. I no longer want to sweat the small stuff, waste precious energy, or tolerate unnecessary drama. I simply want to be happy— optimistic and lighthearted!

8 Things Happy People Refuse to Do

1. Refuse to participate in gossip.
2. Refuse to take on other people's guilt.
3. Refuse to be treated poorly or disrespected.
4. Refuse to be used.
5. Refuse to tolerate other people's bad behavior.
6. Refuse to live by other people's opinions.
7. Refuse to tolerate injustice or unfairness.
8. Refuse to listen to the voice in their heads that says, "I can't do it" or "I'm not good enough."

Guard your energy, guard your time, and guard you heart to prevent being overdrawn, overworked, overcommitted, and over whelmed. Learn how to smile and politely say "No." Then let it go.

40. Replace

Replace . . .

1. **Make good again;**
2. **Put something back where it belongs;**
3. **Substitute something that is broken, inefficient, lost or no longer working effectively with something better.**

Why Replace? Something is broken beyond restoration or repair. The original purpose it served still has value, so it is swapped out with something updated and effective.

"Out with the old and in with the new." There will be times in your life when things simply have to be replaced because they are tired, broken, worn out, harmful, outdated, or irrelevant. Take an inventory of the things which no longer serve your best and highest good so you can replace them with things which do.

Whether it is a belief, a relationship, a wardrobe, a habit, a job, a behavior, or an attitude, finding a better alternative will make the changes in your life sustainable and create more positive outcomes.

When you want to get rid of a bad habit, replace it with a good one. Many of us love our morning cup of java although it can be an unhealthy addiction. When the caffeine buzz wears off, we might crash and feel terrible.

To help break the cycle, choose to replace coffee with a delicious tea—of which there are many varieties to choose. New rituals can make coffee become irrelevant, and create a permanent, healthy change. Try hot apple cider, a probiotic drink, a smoothie, fruit juice or coconut water—all satisfy, but avoid the caffeine buzz.

Any time you remove something from your life, a hole is left behind. Rather than let the old seep back in, choose something better to REPLACE it.

Instead of . . .	Replace it with . . .
Hate and Intolerance	Love, acceptance, and compassion
Pessimism	Optimism
Negativity	Positivity
Bad habits	Healthy alternatives
Gossip	Looking for the best in others
Blame and excuses	Taking responsibility for your role to change your behavior
Being a part of the problem	Becoming a part of the solution
Complaining	Making an effort to correct things
Defending your limitations	Being honest with yourself and changing what is sabotaging you
Letting fear stop you	Finding the courage to get out of your comfort zone and "Just Do It!"
Feeling terrible all the time	Taking better care of your mind, body, and spirit
Tolerating rude behavior	Setting healthy personal boundaries or minimizing interaction
Giving up	Determination and persistence
Taking abuse	Exerting your personal power

"It's never too late. Don't focus on what was taken away. Find something to replace it, and acknowledge the blessings you have."
—Drew Barrymore

41. $\mathcal{R}$egain

"Trust and integrity are precious resources, easily squandered, hard to regain. They can thrive only on a foundation of respect for veracity."
—Sissela Bok

$\mathcal{R}$egain . . .

1. **Succeed in reaching again;**
2. **Get back, recover the use of, retrieve.**

Why Regain? Return that which makes you better. Salvage.

Is there something which you have lost and miss terribly? Are there areas in your life which have slowed down, slipped away, or become confused? Is there something within your character that is valuable, but needs to regain its proper place? Would the quality of your life improve if you regained this certain something?

Whenever I recognize that something important has slipped away, or I feel it slowly diminishing within me, I take deliberate action to secure its place and position.

Moving from Florida to Wisconsin was a drastic change which disrupted my 'norm' in more ways than one. Although it has been a grand adventure for a new experience, my habits, routines, and expectations were knocked off kilter and out of balance. There were odd feelings of displacement. Simple comforts and confidences I once took for granted were tested during the transition. As I have adapted to this new life, I have finally regained my sense of rhythm, purpose, and well-being.

Ask yourself: *Would I be more effective, efficient, productive, or happy if I were to regain an attribute or behavior that has gone by the wayside? Is there something which once was and I yearn for its return?*

What Can You Regain?

- Regain momentum by actively choosing to move forward to make progress.
- Regain traction and stop spinning your wheels.
- Regain trust by demonstrating integrity, respect and honor.
- Regain lost opportunities by pursuing new goals.
- Regain focus by paying attention to detail.
- Regain self-confidence by doing something valuable, even if you are afraid.
- Regain self-respect by doing what is right.
- Regain self-worth by loving and accepting yourself.
- Regain self-esteem by doing your best and being proud of yourself.
- Regain financial stability by being frugal and saving money.
- Regain energy and vibrant health by taking excellent care of YOU!

"Every day you spend drifting away from your goals is a waste not only of that day, but also of the additional day it takes to regain lost ground."

—Ralph Marston

42. Rearrange

"Creativity is a lot like looking at the world through a kaleidoscope. You look at a set of elements, the same ones everyone sees, but then reassemble those floating bits and pieces into an exciting new possibility. Effective leaders are able to."

—Rosabeth Moss Kanter

Rearrange . . .

1. **Put into a new, proper, desired, or convenient order;**
2. **Reshuffle, come to agreement.**

Why Rearrange? Creating spatial serenity and order will impact you in positive ways, both psychologically and physically, that help you become more effective and peaceful.

The shows on HGTV that design, remodel, and renovate living spaces are inspiring and fun. I enjoy seeing the joyful disbelief in people's eyes when they get to see their "space-lift" in their homes for the first time—with everything picture-perfect and organized. Feeling at home, surrounded by beauty and peace, with a sense of order is something we need—not only in the rooms we live in, but in the work we do, and the people that we enjoy.

Straightening, organizing, and shuffling stuff around will open your world to welcome new possibilities. It helps you to clear out the old to bring in the new. When everything is moved to the right space and stored in the right place, you will enjoy more effectiveness, efficiency, and ease.

Ask yourself: *Am I wasting time on frivolous activities? What is easily undone and has proven to be a waste of time? What can I do differently to contribute to the solution of my clutter or organizational problems?*

What Can You Rearrange?

- Your schedule—to use your time more productively.
- Your furniture—to improve the flow of energy and traffic.
- Your relationships. My wise friend Mary Seals once said, "Some of the people in your life need to be thought of like furniture, and you simply have to rearrange the room. Some should be moved to the closet or kicked to the curb."
- Your priorities—to get the most important things done first.
- The pieces of the puzzle—to see which formation comes together to make the picture complete.

One week before the September 11, 2001 tragedy, we wrote a contract to purchase a new home and listed our existing one. It gave us nine months to sell before we had to close on the new one. Plenty of time to get it done, right?

When the Twin Towers fell, everything in America came to a grinding halt— including real estate. After eight grueling months of open houses and no success, we were faced with the scary possibility of double mortgage payments.

Until . . . the day my talented friend Monika walked in. We call her *the house whisperer* for a reason—she has a profound gift for understanding how energy and flow impact our well-being and environment.

She spent the next few hours simply moving through my home and *rearranging* its furniture and accessories. When she was done, everything felt better. Miraculously, the next person who walked in wrote a contract! Consider rearrangement to transform your results.

43. Redefine

*"Are you letting other people define you? If so, you are doing yourself
a great disservice. Plus, you're missing out on what can be a fun,
productive, and yes, even an exciting life . . . You can live
your own life on your own terms. I do!"*

—Francine Ward

Redefine . . .

1. **Give new meaning or different definition to;**
2. **Re-determine boundaries, make distinct, establish a
   clear outline.**

Why Redefine? Create new meanings for the stories in your
life— on your own terms.

It is a human propensity to create labels, assign meanings, and
interpret how you see the world around you. It helps you wrap your
mind around a concept, process information, or achieve clarity and
understanding.

Unfortunately, many of the definitions you may assign
throughout your life can not only narrow your perspective, but
they can prevent you from considering better alternatives.

An "in the box" mentality can be overly self-protective,
short-sighted and small-minded. Many people are so adamantly
defensive of their opinions and being right that it becomes self-
limiting—which blocks new meanings and broader definitions
from flowing in.

When you redefine something, you expand your awareness,
allowing new ideas and thought patterns to emerge. You may
discover new meanings for previously held beliefs. Your new

vantage point can shift your mindset towards positive change and unlimited possibilities.

> *"To manifest prosperity, you have to redefine yourself from a recipient to a co-creator. You have to stop looking for opportunities to present themselves and start creating them."*
>
> —Randy Gage

Instead of thinking . . .	Redefine its meaning . . .
Money is scarce and unavailable.	Money is abundant and I am prosperous.
She was so mean and dismissive to me.	Her behavior is more about her than me.
Getting laid off has been terrifying.	I now have the opportunity to do something I love.
My adult kids will not take my advice.	I am proud my kids are self-reliant.
Getting divorced destroyed my life.	I am now free to discover myself and live my dream.

Changing Lenses

When I lived in Florida it seemed I was constantly buying new sunglasses, as they are essential Southern accessories for proper eye care. One day I tried on a pair of polarized lenses and everything I looked at seemed changed. Colors were more vibrant, shadows were more defined, shapes were crisper, and my perspective of how I saw the world around me shifted.

We can redefine for ourselves how we are seeing the world when we decide to look through a different "lens" or filter. The beauty of doing this is that not only will the things which you see the world change, but it also will transform your emotional and mental interpretation. Begin to pay attention to the lenses you use as you define meaning and truth for yourself.

8 Things in Life to Redefine

1. Redefine failure to make it your best teacher.
2. Redefine change as an opportunity for growth.
3. Redefine your experiences by learning new lessons.
4. Redefine your memories to focus on the good.
5. Redefine your strengths for personal power and resilience.
6. Redefine your faults to embrace your imperfection.
7. Redefine your pain to heal an old wound.
8. Redefine your response to other people's behavior.

As you broaden your perspective, redefine your beliefs, opinions, perceptions, and experiences. The outcomes will enrich your world-view—while all the time, remaining true to you.

44. Reconcile

"The speed of change today is faster than the human psyche seems able to handle, and it's increasingly difficult to reconcile the rhythms of our personal lives with the rapidity of a twenty-four-hour news cycle."

—Marianne Williamson

Reconcile . . .

1. **Bring things together to resolve a matter;**
2. **Appease, make-up, settle, accommodate;**
3. **Bring into harmony, make compatible.**

Why Reconcile? Create peace and order by bringing parts and pieces of your experience back into order, to provide a sense of accuracy, completion, and serenity.

When you reconcile your bank records and checking account, you are bringing everything into balance to confirm that your math matches up. Using this metaphor, apply this same process to your own emotional health and well-being.

Reconciling is about cleaning out your psychic closet. Do you have unresolved issues which are draining your reserves, causing hurt feelings, filling you with regret, or taxing your tenacity? It can be it very difficult to reconcile things which have happened in the past, especially when you can't change the past. Would you like to find peace with them now?

Reconciling Relationships

The areas that *benefit us* to reconcile with another person are highly emotional ones: A divorce. An argument. A disagreement with a colleague. A betrayed confidence. Being let down by someone's lack of dependability. Broken promises. A loved one's refusal to get help.

Relationships, of all shapes and sizes, can be challenging, messy, and can experience rifts for many reasons. A rift is all the more painful if the breakdown has happened with someone you love, trust, and care about.

Is there a person with whom you would like to reunite and resolve a painful or awkward issue (even if the relationship is on a different level or in a "new normal")? What steps can you take to heal relationship struggles, such as the ones mentioned above, or the one you have troubling your heart and mind as you read this?

How Can You Begin to Reconcile?

"Peace is not absence of conflict, it is the ability to handle conflict by peaceful means."

—Ronald Reagan

- Take responsibility for your part and if the shoe fits, wear it.
- Be willing to engage in an honest crucial conversation.
- Share your desire to make things better.
- Let go of the past and focus on your present and the future.
- Apologize and ask for forgiveness if needed.
- Listen to their perspective with patience and respect.
- Forgive their actions and release the struggle.
- Move toward building trust and emotional safety.

Reconciling Your Past with Your Present

Ask yourself: *Am I holding any grudges? Do I need to forgive myself or another person? Am I struggling to release the past? Is it a challenge for me to accept some things I cannot change? Is it difficult for me to appreciate "what is?"*

As an exercise to help you reconcile your present with your past, write down who or what you may resent, why you resent them, what happened, and what your part in the situation was.

Once you've considered all of the different parts in a situation, speak to someone you trust about it, to determine if your perspective can shift. Doing this may enable you to let go of what has been holding you back. Reconciling can help you move forward with acceptance and surrender, rather than berating yourself for what cannot be changed, or berating the other person for not changing.

This has been one of my greatest challenges as I have grieved for what has been lost and wished certain things were still a part of my world. How does one reconcile the need to have a conversation with someone who is no longer alive? How does one reconcile years lost to drama and heartbreak? How does one reconcile being a thousand miles away from your aging mother and adult children to be with the man you love? Believe me—reconciling is a continuous process, with varying degrees of difficulty.

Reading the next chapter, "Release" can help. And you can begin now by thinking of things you are thankful for today. List the incredible gifts, small and large, which bless your life now. Begin with at least one—hopefully, your list of things for which you can be grateful will expand from there.

45. Release

"Even though you may want to move forward in your life, you may have one foot on the brakes. In order to be free, we must learn to let go. Release the hurt. Release the fear. Refuse to entertain your old pain. The energy it takes to hang onto the past is holding you back from a new life. What is it you would let go of today?"

—Mary Manin Morrissey

Release . . .

1. **Liberation, gain freedom from confinement;**
2. **Activity that frees or expresses creative energy or emotion;**
3. **Let go, loosen, free from restraints.**

Why Release? Lighten your load and let go of the burdens in your heart to live a life of freedom, ease, and inner peace.

Dragging around pain and attachments from the past can jeopardize your health, your relationships, and your happiness. It can undermine your motivation, discourage your progress, and make everything in life harder. Ralph Waldo Emerson has been known for saying that "simplicity is the key to happiness."

What can you release to simplify your life, lighten your load, and find more joy? Get real, avoid denial, and thoughtfully address each of the items on the list below to determine which may ring true for you. With each one, say out loud, "I release this" as often as is necessary. Throw it away. Imagine it evaporating. Accept it as gone. Let it go . . .

13 Things to Release

1. Limiting or untrue beliefs.
2. Guilt and regret.
3. Stressed and overwhelmed lifestyle.
4. Fear, worry, and anxiety.
5. Judgment and condemnation.
6. Gossip and speaking ill of others.
7. Old clutter to make room for the new.
8. Bad habits that make you feel terrible.
9. The masks to reveal your authentic self.
10. Resentments, grudges, and lack of forgiveness.
11. Attachment to specific and negative outcomes.
12. Negative thoughts and your stinkin' thinkin'.
13. Control of other people's lives.

A monarch butterfly's healthy development requires continuous release to grow, transform, and thrive. When the caterpillar is hanging upside down, it must release its outer layer of skin for the chrysalis to form. Then, after a period of inner transformation, the newly formed butterfly must break through and release the chrysalis. Once free of its protective cocoon, it spreads its wings, allows the sun to warm and dry them, and then an amazing new journey begins.

Like the butterfly, as you release what weighs you down or holds you back, you will begin a lighter and more peaceful journey.

"Letting go helps us to live in a more peaceful state of mind and helps restore our balance. It allows others to be responsible for themselves and for us to take our hands off situations that do not belong to us. This frees us from unnecessary stress."
—Melody Beattie

46. Renegotiate

> *"Your ability to negotiate, communicate, influence, and persuade others to do things is absolutely indispensable to everything you accomplish in life."*
>
> —Brian Tracy

Renegotiate . . .

1. **Revise the terms of; reexamine and work to create a different result.**

Why Renegotiate? The original negotiation which took place is unbalanced, unfair, or no longer relevant to the parties involved.

Throughout your life, you have been making agreements with yourself and other people. Some of these agreements were mutually beneficial. However, you may find that things which you agreed to in the past are no longer helpful or relevant now. Once you have had a chance to reconsider, you may regret your previous decision and wish to change it. What are you going to do when life changes require you to renegotiate, or when good deals go bad?

How Can You Renegotiate?

- First, acknowledge how and why something isn't working.
- Second, be willing to open the conversation to renegotiate —especially if the other person shares new information which had not previously been considered, or if new information comes to light which needs to be evaluated.
- Third, be invested enough in the relationship or the situation for renegotiation to take place. All of these steps will help you create a more favorable outcome.

Renegotiation applies to a wide variety of situations that may necessitate readdressing details which had previously been agreed upon, such as:

- Serious and life altering renegotiations for labor reform, nuclear arms agreements, health insurance regulations, or free-trade agreements.
- Important personal goals and security: renegotiation of real estate contracts, your salary and benefits, life insurance, college tuition, or the returns on your investments.
- Renegotiation skills also apply to the lighter aspects of life, like getting your children to do chores, rearranging job responsibilities at work, shuffling your time around to be more efficient, or eating a salad instead of a hamburger.

Years ago, we purchased a lakefront home which had been built in the 1950s. Upon reading the home inspection, we discovered that its electrical panel was original and the house would not be insurable until the entire electrical system was updated. As you can imagine, we renegotiated the price to pay for the updates.

I was recently dismayed by the high rates on my cell phone bill. I called the company, shared that I loved doing business with them and had been a loyal customer for over fifteen years. I went on to say that their rates were now over my budget and I was considering leaving to sign on with their top competitor. I kindly requested if they had any solutions for pricing before I moved my business. Taking the initiative for this renegotaion to take place reduced my monthly bill by eighty dollars!

Start thinking about the agreements in your life which no longer serve you, have become burdensome, are no longer fair, or are no longer relevant. It may be time for you to simply renegotiate!

Create a Win-Win

My friend and mentor, Nido Qubein, Ph.D., is the embodiment of dignity, service, grace, brilliance, and success. As the president of High Point University, the chairman of the Great Harvest Bread Company, a board member for many national organizations, a past president of the National Speakers Association, and an international speaker, author, and consultant, he understands the essential art of negotiation. Having arrived in America as a teenager with only fifty dollars in his pocket, he exemplifies hope for the American Dream and has dedicated his life to helping others achieve it.

In his book, *How to Get Anything You Want,* he writes, "The art of negotiating is based on a simple fact—all of us need the cooperation of other people if we are to reach our career and personal goals. And each of us brings to life's bargaining table something that others value." When we seek balance and fairness for all involved, we are more likely to inspire collaboration and build bridges in agreements where everyone wins!

47. Relaunch

"I would say, as an entrepreneur everything you do—every action you take in product development, in marketing, every conversation you have, everything you do—is an experiment. If you can conceptualize your work not as building features, not as launching campaigns, but as running experiments, you can get radically more done with less effort."

—Eric Ries

Relaunch . . .

1. **Reintroduce or restart something;**
2. **Offer, present, or sell a new version of something;**
3. **Set in motion, or make available again.**

Why Relaunch? When a first launch can be improved upon or you want to go bigger, better, and higher than before, boosting your effort will propel you into renewed momentum.

We don't usually think of life or business as a perpetual experiment, but truthfully, life has uncertainty, as do business plans. As people change, our needs and preferences change. As our competition and customers change, so do the demands for our products and services.

For me and likely for you, there comes a time when you may realize that what once worked brilliantly is no longer effective, relevant, or competitive. And as a result, you set out to do a make-over, or design new improvements.

After your innovations, hard work, and implementation, the time comes to reveal your changes. Relaunching is like a coming out party to reveal the new and improved version of what once was.

The book you are now reading was inspired and written quickly.

I had been invited to a public book signing in Florida, which gave me a definite deadline in which to write, edit, publish, and launch. Everything worked out great and my mission was accomplished.

But . . . once I returned home and could relax and breathe, I backed away from the project for a while. After receiving valuable feedback, I was able to reflect and reconsider how I could make this book even better. I read the entire book with fresh eyes and a grateful spirit.

And after a complete re-reading I decided that re-editing, reformatting, and republishing were in order. The second edition is more enriched, profound, and complete. These changes necessitated a relaunch to bring it to the world with greater fanfare and celebration.

9 Things to Relaunch

1. Your new image.
2. Your new website.
3. Your new branding.
4. Your whole business.
5. Your product or service.
6. Your career.
7. A new and improved project.
8. An organizational comeback.
9. Your market positioning.

What, exactly, is it that you need to get going again—inaugurate introduce, or bring into being? To identify it is the first step.

48. Resolution

"Make New Year's goals. Dig within, and discover what you would like to have happen in your life this year. This helps you do your part. It is an affirmation that you're interested in fully living life in the year to come."

—Melody Beattie

Resolution . . .

1.   **A promise to do something;**
2.   **A new course of action.**

Why a Resolution? Declaring what you want in life activates your energy, sets your intention, and helps you build momentum to move forward in the direction of your dreams.

Writing your New Year's resolutions is a great tradition to begin your new year from a position of optimism, positive expectancy, goal setting, and strength. The real magic happens, though, when resolutions become a part of your daily routines, personal habits, and proactive choices.

Some people are so good at telling others what to do with their lives that they get offended when a person doesn't take their advice. Yet, they will not create goals or resolutions for declaring what is important to change in their own lives. Many people associate resolutions with failure because they've broken promises to themselves so many times before that they don't want to fail again. As a result, they avoid setting goals—or making an inner pledge or decree toward a goal.

If you are one of the wise people who does set resolutions, research has shown you are ten times more likely to improve your life when you do. You obviously want to improve your life or you would not be reading this book.

What are you willing to do to make your dreams come true? What time are you willing to invest in creating your best life now? Your resolutions are the key to moving forward in that direction.

Help Your Resolutions Stick

- Be tenacious—stick to your course of action
- Be realistic—one change with reasonable progress
- Be open to time outs—reward with something fun
- Be honest—*never say never!*

Secret Formula for Success

My friend, Tina Hallis, Ph.D., runs the speaking and training firm The Positive Edge (www.thepositiveedge.org). As a positivity expert, she helps people break out of their negative thinking so they can be more positive at work, at home, and with each other.

In her Free Weekly Tips, she shared, "New Year's resolutions are notoriously tough to keep—as is true with almost any goal that requires us to change. Whether we are trying to eat healthier, exercise more, get more organized, or to quit smoking, the odds are against us. Unless . . . we know the secret formula for success:

Passion ÷ Perceived Effort = Success

Tina continues, "The more passion or desire we have and the easier we think it will be, the bigger our chance for success. What is truly great about knowing this formula is the ability to improve our odds by finding ways to *increase* our passion and *decrease* our perceived effort."

49. Renovate to Restore

"A little bit of powder, a little bit of paint, makes a thing of beauty out of a thing that ain't."
—Unknown

Renovate to Restore . . .

1. **Return to its former glory or original condition;**
2. **The process of improving a broken, damaged, or outdated structure;**
3. **Refurbish and make better, bring back to a state of healthy soundness, or vigor.**

Why Renovate to Restore? Bringing something back to life can increase its value, enrich your enjoyment, and improve its usefulness.

Having a deep passion for interior design and creating beauty, I've had the awesome opportunity to renovate and decorate twelve homes, all of which I've lived in. As a renovation junkie, I find great happiness in taking an ugly duckling and making it pretty.

I love using my creative energy to *redo* and *renew* my space to create more value. While residential homes may be the first thing that comes to mind when you think of renovation, it applies to so many more areas which transcend real estate. When you renovate and restore, you take what you already have and make it better.

As a broke college student, I barely had two nickels to rub together. I scraped by, living paycheck to paycheck. With little money to put a home together, I was not too proud to go dumpster-diving, pick up junk on the side of the road, or shop flea markets and garage sales. The thrill of the hunt made the pursuit rewarding and fun.

140

One day, I went into a junk store in Tallahassee and found a small table with great design. It was covered in a hideous greenish mustard-yellow paint. Knowing it was solid mahogany underneath, I offered forty dollars and took it home. Once I stripped away the layers of paint and sanded it down to remove the residue from the past, I coated it with rich layers of stain and varnish to protect it. Till this day, thirty years later, this table is still one of my favorite treasures.

What treasures do you hold, inside or out, which could be renovated or restored? It may well require you to strip off the layers of what is worn and aged, to reveal and rediscover the beauty beneath. Try it today.

Personally, you may owe it to yourself to renovate and restore to deepen your understanding and gain a fresh appreciation for something or someone—or even yourself. To feel happier, more fulfilled, and successful, renovation and restoration removes the layers of *stuff* that have accumulated, helping you move from good, to better—and back to your original best.

What Might You Renovate to Restore?

- Your body
- Your team
- Your home
- Your dreams
- Your business
- Your marriage
- Your community
- Your friendships
- Your environment
- Your faith in humanity

"People, even more than things, have to be restored, renewed, revived, reclaimed, and redeemed. Never throw out anyone."

—Audrey Hepburn

Renew

As you move through the seasons of change and make a deliberate decision to "Review" and "Redo," you will begin to realize just how much power you've had all along to design your life on your terms. As you read through and act on what you have learned in the first two sections, expect emotional space to unlock and open within you, so that you may flourish and bloom again.

Yes, you can create your own reality. However, your ability to RENEW will be more challenging if you stay stuck in limitations and ineffective choices. Clinging to the past and refusing to release what no longer serves you can block your path for personal transformation. Wouldn't you rather allow for renewal, growth, and goodness to spring forth?

Where you may have once felt depleted, tired, or lost, hope can rise again. What may have been a dry and barren landscape can now be renewed, due to your attention and tender loving care.

Your shift in mindset can generate unlimited opportunities for enriching your moments, improving your relationships, and creating something wonderful and new.

Renewal is all around you, inside and out. Whether it is your continuously evolving cell structure, your ever-growing wisdom, your career opportunities, or making new friends—second chances and fresh opportunities abound. On this powerful journey, be and do what you want to attract into your life and you will inevitably have it.

Why Renew?

1. To enjoy higher levels of happiness, satisfaction, peace and well-being.
2. To appreciate how taking good care of yourself helps you take good care of others.
3. To reveal the essentials that prevent burnout.
4. To see all aspects of your life improve.
5. To release the energy, vitality, and stamina to try new things, have new adventures, create new experiences, and live life to its fullest—amidst every change.

50. Refresh

"Rest when you're weary. Refresh and renew yourself, your body, your mind, your spirit. Then get back to work."

—Ralph Marston

Refresh . . .

1. **Renew, freshen again, provide new vigor or energy, reinvigorate, stimulate;**
2. **Recollect, recall, remind.**

Why Refresh? Going "out with the old and in with the new" resets our buttons and revives and prepares us to take on what's next with energy and vigor.

My friend Mona and her family had a fish tank for many years. It had not been cleaned in a while and was getting rather yucky. The fish looked sad, their colors had become dull, and they were not very active. One morning Mona decided, "today is the day" and took the time to refresh it with clean water. After gently moving the fish into a temporary home, she poured out the putrid water. All that was left were the slimy glass walls and poop-filled gravel. And her work began.

Each time she poured in clean water to wash off the gravel, she had to stir up the fish poop to ensure it was removed. Wash, rinse, repeat. After all of the yuck had been stirred up and washed away, she was able to refill the tank with crystal clear, properly conditioned water and return the fish to their home.

When her husband returned home and saw the tank, he asked, "Did you get new fish today?" She replied, "No, they're the same fish, but they just got new water." Quite amazing, because once the gunk was washed away, the fish not only regained their vibrant colors, but their enthusiastic energy returned as well. That's the beauty of being refreshed.

What gunk needs to be washed away and refreshed in your life? What yucky stuff has created a stagnant and negative environment that muddies your waters and depletes your energy? Are you ready to stir things up and make it messy so that you can wash it all away to live a more colorful and vibrant life?

If you know how to "refresh" your computer, you can imagine doing the same in your life. Hitting the refresh button resets your activities, employs changes, and installs updates It brings everything current in seconds.

My friend Joy is a webmaster. Although we live in different cities, we can work on my website simultaneously. She will make changes on her end, which I do not see on my end. Once she has made the improvements, she will say, "Okay, hit refresh." And magically before my eyes, everything she has edited and updated shows up—voilà!

What buttons do you need to push, *or not allow others to mess with or push,* to refresh the changes you want to see in yourself and your world? What needs to be reset to give you a more viable outcome?

"Refresh your mind, clear your problems, and just have fun today."
—Unknown

51. Recharge

"Positive energy is your priceless life force. Protect it. Don't allow people to draw from your reserves; select friends who recharge your energies. I'm not asking you to cut people out of your life, but I am asking you to invest your time with someone else who will push you to be your best. Winners love to see other people win."

—Chalene Johnson

Recharge . . .

1. **Replenish, energize;**
2. **To regain energy and strength.**

Why Recharge? Recharging will jumpstart your energy when you are feeling depleted, running low, or losing luster.

Energy is a valuable commodity—something many people say they don't have enough of in our nonstop culture. Regardless of how energized you may feel when you begin your day, once you have dealt with the hustle and bustle of life, you may feel depleted and drained. It would be great if it never ran down, but that's not realistic.

The battery in my phone works the same way. I plug it in to recharge overnight and by morning it is bursting with 100 percent power. But by the day's end, I'm warned that the charge is low. If I do not tend to it to juice it up again, it will go dead and be of no use to anyone. Your battery doesn't work well when it is "running on empty" and neither do you.

In the book, *The Power of Full Engagement,* Jim Loehr and Tony Schwartz teach that it's not about time management, it's about energy management. Are you managing your energy well and using it for things that matter to you? Do you stop to recharge before you push yourself to critically low levels?

Unplug to Recharge

Have you noticed the insatiable addiction in our society today which people have for screens? Regardless of whether the screen is on a television, a phone, a computer, a smart watch, or an iPad, the obsession is changing how people communicate and interact.

These devices may be necessary for us to stay in touch and stay in business. However, there is a downside. Being plugged in all the time can be an addictive habit—it drains our energy, diverts our focus, wastes our time, and can compromise quality communication, as it diminishes meaningful real life connection with others.

How to Take a Break from Technology

- Unplug and simply turn everything off. It will wait.
- Put electronic devices out of your reach and eyesight for a short while.
- Give your brain a break and silence the information overload.
- Plan for unproductive downtime that allows you to putter.
- Schedule limited times when you check email rather than on a continuous, nonstop basis.

10 Powerful Ways to Recharge Your Days

1. Breathe deeply and oxygenate your body.
2. Drink crystal clear water, with a squeeze of lemon.
3. Get grounded; walk outside and be close to nature.
4. Laugh out loud and find your fun.

5. Take a cold shower.
6. Clean your home, office, or car.
7. Connect in person with a friend or loved one.
8. Learn or teach yourself something new that is for fun.
9. Read or listen to something upbeat and positive.
10. Exercise to work up a good sweat and release mood-lifting endorphins.

"Almost everything will work again if you unplug it, including you."
—Anne Lamott

52. Replenish

"I don't get depressed. When I feel an attack, I withdraw. I disappear, I replenish, and then I come back. I'm not going to wallow in self-pity and not live my life. There are always going to be some falls in life for everybody, no matter what career you have. You have to roll with the punches and keep going."

—Naomi Campbell

Replenish . . .

1. **Fill something which had previously been emptied, resupply.**

Why Replenish? It is no fun to live life on empty.

Replenish sounds and feels like the sheer relief you get from quenching your thirst. Doesn't it feel incredible to enjoy a ice-cold drink on a hot day? Life, like the heat of the sun, can drain your reserves and leave you thirsting for satiation and hydration, can't it? Take the time to renew yourself by finding ways to replenish your body, mind, soul . . . and energy.

Need to refill?

Do you ever feel like you are running on empty? Do you wonder what is missing from your life? What would it take to plug the holes and stop the energy drains? When you see, feel, or think about lack, scarcity, or emptiness, there are ways to plug the drain holes to return to a state of abundance and fulfillment.

"You can't pour from an empty cup." If you don't take care of yourself first, you may not have anything left to take care of others. Even flight attendants instruct: "In the event the cabin loses

pressure, put on your oxygen mask before helping anyone else."

Refuel

What kind of fuel do you fill yourself up with to replenish your energy? You would never pour sugar into your gas tank and expect it to perform at peak levels, would you? Why then are people surprised that they feel so poorly when they have been eating poorly? Your entire life you've heard the phrase, "You are what you eat." It is true indeed. How you choose to refuel your body will impact your quality of life and well-being on cellular, physical, mental, emotional, and spiritual levels.

Healthy Foods

- Fresh, living fruits and vegetables are bursting with nutrition, anti-oxidants, natural enzymes, electrolytes, and energy, all of which serve you well to improve your health and vitality.
- Take a break from refueling with processed food, bad fats, alcohol, white carbs, and empty calories.

Vitamin and Mineral Supplements

- If you think your diet might not be providing you with all of the nutrients needed to optimize your health and energy, you may want to explore additional options for supplementation.

Imagine you are holding a glass of pure water. It is crystal clear and healthy to drink. But then someone drops a drop of black ink into it and the purity is contaminated. Without throwing away the entire glass of water, how can you clean the water to make it pure again? Logic tells you that you have to keep refilling the glass with fresh water until it spills over the brim and the ink is finally flushed away. Filling your life up with the good stuff will help displace the bad stuff, which in turn will replenish and renew your world.

Right now, relax . . . and do *replenish,* for you!

53. Reignite

*"One of the strongest characteristics of genius is the
power of lighting one's own fire."*
—John Foster

Reignite...

1. **Relight, ignite anew;**
2. **Set on fire.**

Why Reignite? Rekindle your passion and your purpose for living well by applying that special spark that gets you 'fired up!'

Passion is that strong feeling of enthusiasm, ecstasy, or excitement which you feel for something or someone. This sizzling desire can light up your soul and fuel your commitment to be persistent in spite of obstacles and unfavorable circumstances. This depth of intrinsic motivation can transform your life unlike anything else and align you with true happiness.

What lights your fire? What gets you so excited that when you are in that state you feel invincible and ready to take on the world? Fan those flames and surround yourself with people who will too. As Rumi wrote, "Set your own fire. Seek those who fan your flame."

Working with Wet Wood

What happens when the passion dies? Are there areas in your life for which you once felt great passion, but the heat has disappeared? If you have ever been in love, you know how the bursting flames of passion can change your perspective on everything. Being on fire and experiencing that flash is glorious, but that degree of heat is rarely sustainable.

As with any other fire, flames must be stoked to keep the fire burning brightly. They must be fed with fuel and oxygen, because if those are denied, cutoff, or squelched, the fire dies. The same happens with most passions and desires in our lives. If we do not feed them with attention, actions, or nurturing, the light may go dim and eventually burn out. *What is the spark of life that is going to get you off the starting block and into action?*

Passion is a very personal emotion which burns deeply from within. However, we sometimes hand this power to control our passion over to others—and in doing so, allow them to throw water on our flames.

Have you had people in your life who stomp on your dreams, invalidate your passion, and rob you of your joy? Now is the time to reclaim your power to rekindle, relight, and reignite your potential.

7 Things to Reignite Your Life

1. Reignite your passion for life and for yourself.
2. Reignite your passion for your work and career path.
3. Reignite your relationships, intimate and otherwise.
4. Reignite your dreams and possibilities.
5. Reignite your physical activities and efforts.
6. Reignite your motivation for making positive changes.
7. Reignite your desire to do your best and try new things.

How Can You Light Your Fire?

- Learn something new to stimulate your ideas.
- Start doing what you love in life and business.
- Be with people who lift you up and raise your energy.
- Listen to your heart and body and do more of what makes you feel great.

- Minimize or eliminate the negative habits, thoughts, interactions with people, or influences that diminish your flame.

"Reignite the fire in your heart. Live on purpose."
—Dawna Markova

Passion Restored

In her inspirational book, *A Passion for Living*, my treasured friend Marnie Tate shares how she has navigated pain, beat stress, and overcome adversity to live a life of joy, passion, and fulfillment. She acknowledges that we all have moments of despair and discouragement and that even the most joyful among us experiences trying times that deplete our energy and dim our light.

She recalls a time when she hit complete exhaustion and burnout while caring for a dying father and running her financial advising business. She found herself in a funk which was hard to get out of. Marnie said, "I had committed to a weekend with some girlfriends in Florida and didn't think I was in the right frame of mind to be with them. I had nothing else to give. I was wrong. After four days of laughing, eating outdoors, walking on the beach, and having no agenda, by the time the weekend was over, my mojo had returned. It was therapy of the grandest kind and my life felt free and glorious again. Friends lift us up when we don't have the energy to fly and I am so grateful for mine. Being able to lean on and depend on our friends when the going gets tough is one of our life's biggest blessings." Joy returned. Passion restored.

54. Reciprocate

"And as we let our own light shine, we unconsciously give other people permission to do the same. As we are liberated from our own fear, our presence automatically liberates others."

—Marianne Williamson

Reciprocate . . .

1. **Act, feel, or give mutually in return;**
2. **Return a compliment, favor;**
3. **Mirror an action, statement or emotion.**

Why Reciprocate? The world is a mirror and when you give without expecting anything in return, you will attract goodness to be returned to you.

The Law of Reciprocity

The "Law of Reciprocity" demonstrates that when we give something from or of ourselves, the receiving party feels an inclination to give back. And in turn, when someone does something nice for you, you naturally want to return the favor. Reciprocity begins a momentum for mutual caring and sweet rewards.

Four Truths of Reciprocity

1. **The Law of Cause and Effect**

   "For whatever a man sows, that he will also reap."

Reciprocity explains how what you give is what you get. The world will mirror back, and reciprocate, whatever you're putting out there—so . . . if you don't like what you're getting, you've got to change what you're giving. Some call it "karma," which promises that the seeds you plant today will determine your harvests tomorrow. The Bible makes many references to this principle.

2. Like Produces Like—Kind Produces Kind.

> *"A good tree cannot bring forth evil fruit, nor*
> *can a corrupt tree bring forth good fruit."*

If you were to plant a grapevine you would get grapes, not oranges. You will harvest according to the seeds you plant. By the same token, the thoughts you think, the things you say, and the actions you take will determine the outcomes you harvest in life. You would be delusional to expect great results from bad actions. Sow your seeds for peace, love, joy, patience, kindness, goodness, and self-control and your harvest will undoubtedly be bountiful and rewarding.

3. You Reap More Than You Sow.

If you plant one tree, it will produce many fruits. One simple action can create a ripple effect with unanticipated impact. Good begets good and has a multiplier effect to spread more good. Bad begets bad, leaving collateral damage and destruction in its wake. Choose wisely, for the seeds you sow will grow and multiply.

4. Be Patient.

> *"But we should not lose heart in well-doing, for in*
> *due season we shall reap, if we do not faint."*

It takes time to reap what you have sown to enjoy the rewards of your plantings. You would not expect a seed to produce fruit the next day. Yes, patience . . . always a challenge. While you might not see immediate results, try to rest patiently in knowing that you have been putting out your best and doing your best, and the rest will follow.

Reciprocation is more than a flow of giving shared between two people. Instead of holding on tightly to something, your hand is wide open. The universe operates through dynamic exchange and the magic happens when the giver gives without expecting back.

8 Easy Ways to Reciprocate

1. A kind word
2. A generous deed
3. An act of service
4. Respect for differences
5. Healthy communication
6. Emotional safety
7. A favor without attachments
8. Love and affection

On Becoming a Giver

"Take time to appreciate employees and they will reciprocate in a thousand ways."
—Bob Nelson

"It is better to give than to receive," is a lifetime philosophy for the givers who have the generosity of spirit to give without expecting anything in return. Through acts and deeds of generosity, we are able to create happy, fulfilled, and deeply meaningful lives, as we contribute to the well-being of another life.

55. *Regenerate*

"Regeneration can come only through a change of heart in the individual."
—Henry Williamson

Regenerate . . .

1. **Reconstitute, revive, bring into existence again;**
2. **A renewed existence, activity, or growth;**
3. **Reformed or reborn, especially in a spiritual or moral sense.**

Why Regenerate? Breathing new life into your thinking, activities, and relationships will create fresh ideas for innovative ways of living.

Step back and take a candid look at your life—your relationships, your career, and your attitude. Are there areas where you would like to infuse a new perspective to shift your current reality? Whether it's in your office, your home, your goals, or your finances, what would you like to regenerate that would bring you up to your next level for inspired solutions and satisfaction?

Some people contend that there are no new ideas and everything under the sun has already been created. Thankfully, innovation and regeneration continue to prove otherwise. New and amazing innovations are born every day from the regeneration of ideas and creativity. How can you create something completely brand new using your current resources?

What Can You Regenerate?

- Old concepts to birth new ideas.

- Creativity for out-of-the-box innovation.
- Support, participation, and buy-in.
- Fun and light-heartedness.
- Muscle mass and strength.
- A sense of gratitude and appreciation.
- Clarity to gain a clearer understanding.
- An old idea and give it new meaning.
- Solutions and answers for problems and questions.
- The old and tired, to make it new again.
- Interest in something for which people have lost their enthusiasm or have stopped paying attention.

Nature Knows the Secret

"In biology, regeneration is the process of renewal, restoration, and growth that makes genomes, cells, organisms, and ecosystems resilient to natural fluctuations or events that cause disturbance or damage. Every species is capable of regeneration, from bacteria to humans."

—Wikipedia

Many species in the animal kingdom can survive and thrive because of their ability to regenerate. Their ability to repair and regrow lost body parts enables them to stay strong and flourish. Whether it is a deer re-growing antlers, a lizard re-growing its tail, a shark re-growing teeth, or a starfish re-growing an arm, regeneration is a natural occurrence for replacing what has been lost.

When things in your life have become lost or damaged,
keep the hope that they can and will be regenerated and restored.
"Love it. Do it. Be in it. Become it until it regenerates in your legacy."

—Goitsemang Mvula

56. Reinvent

"People who cannot invent and reinvent themselves must be content with borrowed postures, secondhand ideas, fitting in instead of standing out."

—Warren Bennis

Reinvent...

1. **Bring back into existence;**
2. **Create anew or makeover completely.**

Why Reinvent? You have the freedom to modify your identity to live the life you've always wanted, and be the person you want to be. No one is just like you . . . be an original.

We are all a work in progress. From the day we are born and beyond, we are in a continuous state of renewal and reinvention. You don't find yourself, you create yourself. Reach for more!

Why Reinvent?

- You have reached a new stage in life and you get to design a new adventure. Start with writing a "bucket list."
- You're unhappy with the status quo and want to make changes to what has become boring. Shake it up!
- The way you have been doing things is no longer interesting or exciting. Become curious, and learn how you can add more excitement and interest to what has become unpleasant or is out-of-whack.
- You have a great foundation and the resources to work with and want to rearrange the pieces to create something new. Don't wait. What do you want to create in your life? Take a chance!

Life is a Daring Adventure and She's Not Done Yet!

My dear friend Mary Helen Conroy is a reinvention life coach who specializes in helping middle-aged clients reinvent their lives to optimize their next chapter. After experiencing decades filled with her own life changes, she discovered winning ways to move beyond her transitions through reinvention. Using her *Reinvention Portfolio Process*, she helps clients develop adventures to make retirement the best years of their lives.

She shares that reinvention isn't only about change and transition, but about deciding what you want to be when you grow up and creating an action plan to live your dreams—whatever your age.

When Reinvention Meets Resistance

"Don't judge me by my past. I don't live there anymore."
—Unknown

Have there been times when you earnestly wanted to make a change, but the people around you resisted it because you were disrupting their perception of you? Or perhaps someone whom you care about did not support you because "the new you" made them feel jealous, uncomfortable, or insecure?

Another friend of mine reunited with a life coach with whom she had worked with for three years. As they were walking, he tried to project his opinions onto her about who she had previously been. He was really challenging her on something which he believed about her, and he wanted her in agreement.

She began to laugh and said, "Excuse me, but you're not talking to me. You're talking to the me of three years ago. I'm not that person anymore." He said, "Yes you are because you did this, and this, and this." She said, "When taken out of context, I can see how you feel that way. But placed in context, it no longer applies." I'm glad she had the confidence in her current self to not allow her former life coach to take her backwards.

Making room for your new changes, pursuits, and interests might require other people to change their perception of how to embrace the new you. Some will, some won't.

My friend Deborah bought her new house from an owner who was selling because he had experienced a stroke. Having been reminded of how short life can be, he had decided to move to California to reinvent his life and enjoy a new adventure. His friends were baffled and did not support his decision.

They would ask, "What are you thinking? You don't know anyone there!" Sometimes it takes a major crisis or a wake-up call for us to reinvent our life and create a new experience regardless of how other people feel about it.

Humans naturally resist change because it requires adapting which can be very uncomfortable. When people around you do not support your personal growth and development, it doesn't mean you are on the wrong path or that you must listen to them. Just because someone continues to judge you from where you were doesn't mean you have to stay there. It can be hard to not receive support from those who matter most. But as in the animal world, if it becomes necessary for survival, you may have to change your place and position in the herd, or find a new pack altogether.

"A successful reinvention doesn't happen when you hate the person
you are. It happens when you love yourself enough to
believe that you can do better and deserve better."
—Dr. Phil McGraw

57. Repurpose

"Uncommon thinkers reuse what common thinkers refuse."
— J.R.D. Tata

Repurpose . . .

1. **Use in a new form or fashion;**
2. **Recycle, reuse;**
3. **Create a new intention, end, aim, goal.**

Why Repurpose? Finding new and better uses for assets you already have will save you money, time, energy, and sanity.

I grabbed onto the concept of repurposing with both hands and all ten toes during my lean financial years. Many resources you already have access to can become tools for your survival and resilience.

In the movie *Gone with the Wind*, Scarlet O'Hara's mansion has been ransacked, the fields burned, and she has lost everything. Well . . . almost. Still wanting to impress her man and demonstrate a flair of elegance and strength, she has Mammy make her a beautiful gown from the green velvet drapes in her home. Her dress became a symbol for survival and resilience. (And Carol Burnett repurposed this scene for comedy in her hit TV show from the 60s and 70s.)

When you find a new purpose for an old thing, it may not be so dramatic. But having the mindset to be so creatively inclined is a wise means for renewal. Rather than wasting or eliminating items which you don't currently need or use, find another use that will serve you better.

Thoughts

Repurposing can be applied to more than physical things. Consider repurposing your thoughts. While the gremlin in your head may be trying to keep you safe, it can also make you stay small and play safe as it tries to keep you from getting hurt.

Tell that never-ending warning voice: "Thank you. I appreciate you helping me and trying to protect me, but I don't need it anymore. This is what I really need your help with _____. Would you please stand guard to make sure that you support me and my responsibilities to do this instead?" What persistent thoughts do you have that would serve you better if you repurposed them to help you rather than hinder you?

Talents

I once had a coaching client who was an eloquent political speaker, however, that particular platform did not bring him joy. I encouraged him to expand and repurpose his talent for inspiring and motivating others to live his passion, rather than continuing to jump through the hoops of politics.

We see many people, who upon retirement, will pursue new opportunities in which they can utilize their strengths and be of service, even if it is in a completely unrelated field.

Ask yourself: *What strengths and talents can you put to a different use for creating a new endeavor, participating in a passionate quest, or put to good use to make a few extra dollars?*

Content

When I write content for my books, it is not for the sole purpose of publishing a book. Once I have converted my material into content for the book, it can then take on many new forms and have various applications—revision progresses to the point of reinvention and its purpose is expanded. And it's a welcome relief to realize there's no need to recreate the wheel for additional content when I can re-purpose the final content of my books by turning it into blogs, social media posts, podcasts, quote cards, and more. Repurposing helps me save incredible amounts of time, while exponentially growing my message and impact.

> *"Our goal becomes our purpose. What we find along the way, we*
> *repurpose to reach that goal. The repurpose of an old thought, idea,*
> *or memory to a new purpose is the height of creativity."*
>
> —Steve Supple

58. Restart

*"Starting all over again is not that bad . . . .
You get another chance to make things right."*

— Ryan Ferreras

Restart . . .

1. **Set in motion again, get going, rouse;**
2. **Spring forward, jumpstart, begin again.**

Why Restart? It is time to get unstuck from the muck and get moving again.

Things sometimes come to a grinding halt without warning! Do you ever feel that you've been stopped dead in your tracks? That you've fallen and you can't get up? That you're stuck in a rut or wading in muck? Paralysis, inertia, and apathy can be disabling and disempowering. What is it going to take for you to restart your engine and get moving again? Life rewards action, so rev up your resilience and get rolling. Have the fearlessness to start again.

Cooling off Period

When an engine runs hot, it is wise to turn it off for a while to let it cool down. You might even have to go as far as to douse it with water or cap off the coolant. It is wise to take precautions before restarting the engine to ensure its safety, stability, and recovery.

Changes in your own life can occur as an unsettling shock to your system and it's best to cool down before making any new decisions. Before you pull yourself completely out of the muck on your restart to recovery, it is wise to create the space to get grounded. Release the old, feel the painful emotions, process the grief, finish off the fear, and accept the changes which have happened to you before starting out on the road again.

What Requires a Restart?

- Leaving home for the first time.
- Starting from scratch after bankruptcy.
- Moving into a new home or neighborhood.
- Starting over after a divorce or the loss of a loved one.
- Creating a new life when your children have left home and your nest is empty.
- Changing careers and working in a different town, industry, or environment.
- Feeling a sudden loss of identity and purpose after retirement.

Rebooting

When your computer gets overwhelmed and overloaded, its ability to function well is diminished. A rebooting may be needed to improve its performance and increase its capacity. It gives it a chance to clean out the old, restart all systems to the reliable default, install the latest updates, and apply the new changes the user indicates they want. Likewise, sometimes we would do well to "reboot."

Ask yourself: *As I read above the processes that occur when a computer undergoes a 'reboot,' what adjustments would benefit me in a personal rebooting?*

Getting a Jumpstart

Do you ever feel as if your own battery is drained and lifeless?

When you're having trouble getting your engine started again, you might need to call for help. Your help may arrive by calling a wise friend, hiring a consultant or coach, talking to a counselor, hearing a motivational talk, reading a great book, or joining a new group. Or, a jumpstart may come through to you as answered prayer. Regardless of who, how, or what it is going to take, jumpstart your journey so that you can *start moving* in the direction of your greater good and your dreams.

"No matter how hard the past, you can always begin again."
— Buddha

59. Reunite

"We may not have to have it all together, but together we have it all."
— Unknown

Reunite . . .

1. **Have a reunion, unite again;**
2. **Bring together after a period of separation or disunity.**

Why Reunite? We are stronger together than apart—and life is simply better when we move through it together.

Are you separated from loved ones? Has it been a long time since you saw people whom you care about? Are you depleted by disagreements among those around you? Are you challenged by people who are not working together in the workplace to achieve a common mission or a higher goal?

A rich solution to solve any of these challenges is to seek and find ways to reunite and unify. Whether you reunite physically, emotionally, or intellectually in shared goals, passion, or purpose, the reunion of separate pieces fortifies the whole. This reuniting is not just about bringing people together, but it brilliantly extends to unifying ideologies, priorities, goals, attitudes, and perceptions. Getting everyone on the same page enables us to get more done— and then at other times, we reunite with friends or loved ones just for fun!

Team Unity

"I would rather have 1% of the efforts of 100 people than 100% of my own."
—Unknown

172

Every time I speak to a team or organization, it is my greatest hope and intention that the words I share will inspire them to work well together. When teams pull together to serve a higher purpose, their synergy builds momentum and helps everyone head in the right direction. A unified team is a force to be reckoned with. When people pull together, have each other's backs, and strive to achieve a clearly defined purpose, the culture is empowered to produce extraordinary outcomes.

What can be Reunited?

- Family.
- Friends.
- Work teams; sports teams.
- Colleagues.
- Your words, deeds, and actions with your greater purpose.
- Ideas, opinions, and principles which help bring clarity, solutions, and progress.

Be willing to create the space, the place, and the effort to reunite with people who matter to you—personally or professionally— with whom you share a common purpose. Network and be willing to reach out to people to keep your connections strong. Enjoy the rewards of being together.

> *"I like to see people reunited, I like to see people run to each other,*
> *I like the kissing and crying, I like the impatience, the stories that the*
> *mouth can't tell fast enough, the ears that aren't big enough, the eyes*
> *that can't take in all the change, I like the hugging, the bringing*
> *together, the end of missing someone."*
> —Jonathan Safran Foer

60. Rediscover

"If we are to go forward, we must go back and rediscover those precious values—that all reality hinges on moral foundations and that all reality has spiritual control."

—Martin Luther King, Jr.

Rediscover . . .

1. **Discover something once again;**
1. **Find something which has been lost, forgotten, or ignored.**

Why Rediscover? Life is filled with wonder, adventure, and unlimited possibilities when you open yourself up to find and explore, learn and grow.

While adapting to change as you move forward through life, there are things which can get lost along the way. You may never have intended for this to happen, especially if they made you happy and brought you joy.

What Can You Rediscover?

- Rediscover your purpose and passion—do what you dream.
- Rediscover your strengths and talents—be the hero or heroine of your own story.
- Rediscover your childlike wonder—the optimism and innocence.
- Rediscover the magic in the moment—laugh and smile.
- Rediscover the beauty around you—through sunshine, nature, and fun.

Somewhere between handling challenges, taking care of business, and juggling responsibilities, you may have lost pieces of yourself which you long to unearth and rediscover. Perhaps they were buried and forgotten long ago. Rediscovering is more than just being reminded of these golden treasures. It is being able to excavate your riches, pull them out, polish them off, and allow them to shine again—for you to act on and believe, and for others to see.

Rediscover the Value of Like-Minded Friends

I celebrate diversity and admire the unique differences we all bring. The world offers such a variety of people that there are always ways to grow and learn beyond your own paradigm. There is also joy in the rediscovery of having like-minded friends with whom you can relax and securely let down. This like-mindedness feels like you have found your tribe—your home—a place where you fit in, especially when you have been without it for a while.

When you align yourself with people who think like you and create like you, the sky is the limit for achieving your goals. It promotes easy companionship.

In the words of Tony Robbins, "When you are with the right person, relationships don't take a lot of work." Haven't you noticed that being with like-minded people makes communication easy and effortless? It is a nice rediscovery when you surround yourself with people who understand and bring out the best in you.

5 Ways to Rediscover Your Joy

1. Practice gratitude—it will help you *reframe.*
2. Do things which you used to find fun—they will *reawaken* the dormant.
3. Listen to your intuition and gut feelings—they will help

you reconnect to your truth.

4. Remember a time when you were at your happiest; make choices and go places that bring recovery and rediscovery.

5. Pay attention to what makes you feel good and bad—this will help you discover when and what to *replace* and what to refuse.

"One of the advantages of being disorganized is that one is always having surprising discoveries."

—Winnie the Pooh (A.A. Milne)

61. Relax & Relieve

"We will be more successful in all our endeavors if we can let go of the habit of running all the time, and take little pauses to relax and re-center ourselves. And we'll also have a lot more joy in living."

— Thich Nhat Hanh

Relax . . .

1. **Loosen up, unwind, take it easy;**
2. **Make less tense, firm, or rigid;**
3. **Bring relief from the effects of tension or anxiety.**

Relieve . . .

1. **Reduce or remove something, such as pain or an unpleasant feeling;**
2. **Make a problem less serious.**

Why Relax and Relieve? Relaxing will relieve much of what ails you as your health, mindfulness, and well-being are restored—which in turn will promote a longer and more enjoyable life.

It is a stressful world out there and your ability to navigate, handle, and reduce that stress will greatly impact your health, well-being, and happiness. Learn how to relax and find relief regularly so that you are not consumed by the demands of an unrelenting world.

Ask yourself: *What might I need relief from? Anxiety? Depression? Stress? Work? Drama? Negative people? Physical pain? Agitation? Responsibilities? Being overworked and underpaid? Information overload? Interpersonal relationships?*

The Center for Healthy Minds at the University of Wisconsin has become the global leader for understanding how our minds and emotions impact our well-being. Researchers have found that mindfulness, defined as *a mental state achieved by focusing one's awareness on the present moment while calmly acknowledging and accepting one's feelings, thoughts, and bodily sensations,* can be used as a therapeutic technique. I suggest that you recognize and utilize mindfulness as an integral part of maintaining your health, vitality, and resilience.

There was a time when "motivation, positivity, and inspiration" simply described being positive and having an optimistic attitude. Science, however, can now prove that these mental states can improve the quality of life, and add to longevity, for everyone.

13 Ways to Relax and Relieve

What relaxes you? What works for one person may stress another person out, or bore them to tears. Soft music and candlelight may inspire one person, and put another to sleep. Seek your pleasure and discover healthy ways in which you can relax and rest.

1. Practice mindfulness and be still. Become aware and embrace the present moment.
2. Breathe deeply, clear your mind of incessant thoughts.
3. Reground yourself and spend time in nature.
4. Exercise, stretch, and move your body to release stress.
5. Enjoy a favorite hobby like walking, swimming, painting, kayaking, golfing, or fishing.
6. Entertain your brain by reading, doing crossword puzzles,

Sudoku, chess, etc.

7. Participate in hypnosis, guided meditations, or yoga.
8. Get a massage, a facial, or a pampering session.
9. Replace your own thoughts with TED Talks, inspirational seminars, scripture, or affirmations.
10. Laugh out loud and find your fun to release happiness hormones and elevate your mood.
11. Watch uplifting movies, videos, or TV shows.
12. Unplug from life, computers, obligations, and busy-ness.
13. Nourish your body with living foods and nutrition.

> *"There is more to life than increasing its speed."*
> —Mohandas K. Gandhi

62. Re-engage

"We are at our very best, and we are happiest, when we are fully engaged in work we enjoy on the journey toward the goal we've established for ourselves. It gives meaning to our time off and comfort to our sleep. It makes everything else in life so wonderful, so worthwhile."

—Earl Nightingale

Re-engage . . .

1. **Re-attract the attention or involvement of;**
2. **Get more involved or begin participating;**
3. **Re-establish a meaningful connection or contact.**

Why Re-engage? Enjoying living life at its fullest, both with yourself and with others, requires involvement and participation.

Being fully engaged in life is a conscious decision. People who choose to dissociate can lose their enthusiasm to even put forth the effort. They disengage for a variety of reasons—boredom, disinterest, rejection, apathy, overwhelm, or exhaustion. Once a person begins to disengage, their apathy can bleed over into other areas of their life, which further disconnects them from what and who might actually bring them joy.

If this has happened to you, there is hope for getting back in the game again. To move from disengagement to re-engagement, ask the right questions to find the right answers.

Ask yourself: *Am I willing to look at my life to figure out why I'm doing what I am doing and why I'm not doing what I need to for involvement in meaningful connections and activities?*

7 Questions to Ask Yourself to Re-engage

1. Are you living a balanced life? (Is anything taking up too much of your time, or do you need to initiate any change?)
2. Is your work meaningful and making a difference? (Does it energize you or deplete you?)
3. Do you desire to change and be engaged again? (What can you identify that might be standing in the way?)
4. Do you tend to be an optimist or a pessimist? (Looking for the best in yourself, others, and situations?)
5. Do you set goals and have dreams? (Do you have active direction and hopefulness for future outcomes?)
6. Do you pursue new opportunities? (If not, what can you see yourself doing to help make that happen?)
7. What are you willing to do about it? It's up to you!

While *Release the Power of Re³* is bursting with ideas for you to create positive change and transformation, you will also find profound ways to personally re-engage. Among my favorites are:

- Lighten with laughter and find humor in simple things. Be playful, silly, and find your fun.
- Step up, volunteer, participate, and get involved.
- Do something nice for another person.
- Share your heart; tell others you love and appreciate them.
- Read uplifting and inspirational books for empowering ideas.
- Teach yourself something new and embrace learning.
- Choose to be positive.
- Engage in activities that fulfill, excite, and delight you.

Engagement in the Workplace

When employees are fully engaged, they produce, contribute, and perform at higher levels. As a result, active, engaged team players bring much more value to their companies. One of our greater challenges in the workplace today, however, is the serious level of disengagement among the staff. It is a troubling symptom of isolation, occurring for many reasons.

The disengagement statistics are alarming and it is costing employers billions of dollars a year. Great leaders who are challenged with such disengagement must take swift action for re-engaging their people if they hope to keep their culture strong and viable.

10 Ways to Re-engage Your Workplace

1. Personally get to know and care about your people.
2. Create an emotionally safe culture where employees feel valued, respected, and appreciated.
3. Use healthy communication skills with active listening.
4. Invest in your people with training and coaching for personal and professional development.
5. Praise in public, criticize in private.
6. Communicate a clear vision, shared goals, and expectations.
7. Create a culture where hidden talents can be cultivated.
8. Catch people doing things right and say "thank you."
9. Involve others in change initiatives to gain buy-in.
10. Build and nurture team unity and spirit.

"To be fully engaged, we must be physically energized, emotionally connected, mentally focused and spiritually aligned with a purpose beyond our immediate self-interest."

—Jim Loehr

63. Rewrite

"Life may not always fall into neat chapters, and you may not always get the satisfying ending you're looking for, but sometimes a good explanation is all the rewrite you need."

—Harlan Coben

Rewrite . . .

1. **Alter your writing to create a new story;**
2. **Rewrite as to make fit to suit a new or different purpose, revision.**

Why Rewrite? Shift the narrative of your life to become the positive vision you hold for it and watch as it unfolds in empowering, fulfilling, and joyous ways.

You are the author of your own life story. You have the leading role and get to determine how you interact with your supporting cast and the other characters. As in literature, your life may also be a mixture of drama, comedy, adventure, mystery, tragedy, and romance, full of plot twists, suspense, and heroes and villains.

Without realizing it, we can allow the events of our lives to write our story for us, rather than taking the deliberate action necessary to write our own story our way. Engage your imagination and ask yourself how you would like for your story to change. Which archetypes are helpful and which are harmful? What will it take to further love and appreciate your life story, and create the happy endings you desire?

My friend Kelly Swanson is an award-winning storyteller, comedian, and motivational speaker. She inspires audiences worldwide with tools for crafting their best life stories for making a positive impact, connecting with others, and expanding their influence. She shares that "Personal stories reveal something about you, personally. When we know you as a person, we connect to you. Now we will listen to what you say."

Ask yourself: *What is it that I want to say that will bring meaning and positive results to those who hear me—or to how I hear myself?*

Please read the following quote twice . . . and slowly.

"Owning our story can be hard but not nearly as difficult as spending our lives running from it. Embracing our vulnerabilities is risky but not nearly as dangerous as giving up on love and belonging and joy—the experiences that make us the most vulnerable. Only when we are brave enough to explore the darkness will we discover the infinite power of our light."

—Brene' Brown

Next, ask yourself the following questions inspired by Brene' Brown's quote. After answering each question, if needed, ask yourself, "What can I do to *rewrite* this?"

- What am I not taking responsibility for in my life?
- What am I running from?
- Where do I feel most vulnerable and unhappy?
- What have I given up on?
- How would I like to be more brave?
- In a perfect world, what would my life look like?

Now, celebrate as you rewrite to release your innate power to create positive changes for yourself.

64. Replant

*"The future may be rooted in the past,
but you can always uproot and replant."*

—Unknown

Replant . . .

1. **Plant again or anew;**
2. **Sow new seeds, ideas, connections.**

Why Replant? Finding a healthier place for your roots to grow will allow you to blossom to your full potential.

Replanting will help you sow the desires of your heart. And if your plantings don't take, don't give up. Simply plant, plant, and replant as needed. Do this until your precious seed germinates, lodges into place, and you see the evidence of growth.

When you have failed at something, try again. When your hopes and expectations have fallen through, don't give up. When you have lost something which you once valued, seek to replace it. Replanting is the natural process to spur growth and renewal.

To Ensure Future Benefit

Florida is home to thousands of acres of orange groves. Every few years there will be a winter freeze that hits so hard it destroys thousands of trees. The grove owners have no other choice but to remove the dead trees and replant their groves with new trees if they hope to stay in business. The replanting ensures future crops and prosperity.

Plant something today that your future self will thank you for.

As with any seed or plant, follow these steps: Don't bury it too deep, give it room to grow, provide the nutrition it needs to thrive, understand it may take longer than expected, and realize the fruit might taste different than you imagine.

What Can You Replant?

- A dream which has died inside.
- An affirming belief in yourself or others.
- An idea that can grow into something big.
- A suggestion to guide your team for improvement.
- Roots to Grow and Wings to Fly.

"Choose to bloom wherever you are planted."
—Unknown

A plant can become root bound when it is living in an environment which constricts its expansion. Without the room to grow and expand, its roots can become tangled, mangled, and strangled. A plant can only grow relative to the size of its limited confines thereby stifling its potential.

Once the plant is moved to a larger pot, however, it is given the space, place, and freedom to grow. While the uprooting may at first cause a shock to its system, it finds a way to adapt to its new home. Transplanting will help it grow in ways which would not have happened otherwise. It allows for expansion and creates the opportunity to increase its size, strength, vitality, influence, and beauty.

You may have experienced a similar situation, either because a life change has uprooted your world from what you once knew, or because your environment was limiting your personal growth and expansion. Apply these standard planting principles to areas in life, work, and self where you would like to stimulate new and revitalized growth. It is in the replanting or transplanting that you can do some of your best work and expand your roots to grow, thrive, and flourish.

Whether you need to change places physically or metaphorically, replanting and putting down new roots will encourage new possibilities.

65. Reactivate

"The way to activate the seeds of your creation is by making choices about the results you want to create. When you make a choice, you activate vast human energies and resources, which otherwise go untapped."

—Robert Fritz

Reactivate . . .

1. **To restore something for the better;**
2. **To impart new life, energy, or vigor.**

Why Reactivate? *Turn on and tune in* to your hopes and dreams—stimulate and spark your gifts and skills into actions that turn your intentions into reality.

Life Rewards Action

An object in motion tends to stay in motion, so if you want to go places and do great things, get moving! Although the desires of your heart may be lying dormant for a reason or a season, now may be the perfect time to reactivate them and infuse them with life.

Activating Your Intentions

Your intentions direct your attention. Deepak Chopra once shared that "Intention is the starting point of every dream. It is the creative power that fulfills all of our needs, whether for money, relationships, spiritual awakening, or love." If you earnestly want to create positive change in your life, start by setting a conscious intention to propel you in that direction and then take action.

However, you must align your subconscious mind with your intention, or you may discover that achieving your goals is a continuous struggle. Since your subconscious mind does not distinguish between "real" events and "synthetic" reality, you can influence, through the power of your imagination, how information is received, retrieved, and activated by your deeper mind.

By consciously setting an intention and then programming the subconscious mind, you will increase the likelihood of attaining your goals. To help bridge your conscious intention with your subconscious mind, imaginatively connect your objective with your senses of sight, sound, touch, taste, and smell, or with a symbol, memory, or feeling that represents your desired outcome.

4 Ways to Activate Your Intentions by Connecting Your Conscious and Subconscious

1. In your mind's eye, *see* yourself in a future scene enjoying your feeling of accomplishment. Be there—allow the details to fill in and become your present moment.
2. As you *listen* to your favorite music, allow it to become the musical score for the story of your success and notice how it makes you feel. Ride the waves of music in celebration.
3. *Feel* yourself floating effortlessly above a scene in the future, watching yourself as you perform masterfully, expressing confidence, competence, and joy. Notice how you feel. Now anchor that *feeling* by squeezing your wrist.
4. *Imagine* that you are walking down a path through a forest sanctuary. It is peaceful, beautiful, vibrant, and alive. You hear water splashing and gurgling nearby as if in a song of celebration. As you arrive at a pool of clear, sparkling water you *look* into your reflection and smile.

Get clear and specific in sensory detail to experience what it feels like to succeed—as if it has already happened. Your subconscious mind will accept the virtual experience as fact and then be on board with the conscious decisions you implement.

66. Recommit

"Productivity is never an accident. It is always the result of a commitment to excellence, intelligent planning, and focused effort."
—Paul J. Meyer

Recommit . . .

1. **To commit again, confide, or entrust;**
2. **Make a new promise.**

Why Recommit? Asserting your dedication to a project, a goal, a person/people, or yourself through reaffirmation and action will propel you along the course you have chosen.

Have you ever made a commitment for which you felt conviction or passion at the time in which it was made, yet as time went by, you lost interest, lost passion, got distracted, or found something else which would result in a greater reward? If your commitments have waivered, recommit yourself to fulfill your promises and do the right thing.

What Can You Recommit To?

- Recommit to your relationships.
- Recommit to your goals.
- Recommit to your education.
- Recommit to a spiritual path.
- Recommit to your promises.
- Recommit to your sobriety.
- Recommit to doing your best.
- Recommit to your health, wellness, and exercise plan.

Lack of Commitment

Broken commitments can lead to disappointment, betrayal, loss of respect for yourself and others, and damage to your reputation; unfortunately, with a snowball effect. Often times this will happen when a person has made a half-hearted commitment by trying to make other people happy. It's not surprising when a forced commitment lacks dedication. No wonder it may inevitably lead to broken promises. Evaluate to consider if you have made a commitment in integrity and decide whether to drop it or reinforce it; make appropriate adjustments keeping in mind how you might avoid or repair any damage that might occur to others.

Over Commitment

A friend shared with me how she was serving on several work projects. Her coach challenged her as to how many she felt obligated to but didn't enjoy. She guessed four, but after further review, realized there were seven, yes, seven! Her coach reminded her that she was taking up space and preventing someone else from stepping in who was fully committed and could bring greater contributions. She cheerfully, without guilt, resigned from all seven of her commitments, enabling her to recommit her energy towards her skills and passions, which naturally began to take her where she really wanted to go.

> *"It was character that got us out of bed, commitment that moved us into action, and discipline that enabled us to follow through."*
>
> —Zig Ziglar

67. Rebirth

"In the last few years, losing my father, going through a divorce, and not getting some jobs I really wanted, is making me a much more interesting person, I think. This all really does feel like a rebirth, a new chapter."

—John Stamos

Rebirth . . .

1. **Renaissance, resurgence, revival;**
2. **A renewed existence, activity, or growth;**
3. **The action of reappearing or starting to flourish or increase after a decline.**

Why Rebirth? Literature, philosophy, psychology, and spiritual traditions are replete with examples of the power of being born again to a new way of being to transform and enhance our experience of life.

Rebirth can be one of your most significant moments of transformation. While it is a mystical experience in spirituality and religion, the concept of rebirth represents the metamorphosis which is possible in everyone's lives. For many it is the ultimate renewal. It is transformative and restores, and is for some, miraculous.

Butterflies are the symbol of rebirth, hope, new beginnings, and transformation. When a caterpillar goes into its chrysalis and re-emerges as a butterfly, it experiences a complete process of rebirth. It demonstrates how a living breathing organism is transformed into a completely new creation, yet has the same DNA. Every stage of development is necessary to bring a butterfly to its predetermined, glorious manifestation.

The rebirthing process is not without pain. When the butterfly is beginning to emerge reborn from the chrysalis, it has to fight to get out. The struggle is real and necessary. If you were to take a small knife to help create an opening in the chrysalis for the butterfly to escape, its existence would be short-lived. It is its struggle which strengthens its wings and fortifies it to thrive so that it can fly far and wide.

You too may go through stages of development which can lead to rebirth. Your greatest struggles may be your best teachers, in which you develop great wisdom and personal strength. Such dramatic growth experiences help lead you to your true purpose and personal renaissance.

Breaking out of your comfort zone, shedding the old layers, and stretching your potential may or may not help you become your best self, but the process will enable you to spread your wings and take flight.

Quietly consider where you desire rebirth—physically, emotionally, or spiritually.

"We all hope for breakthrough rebirth moments."
—Dane Cook

68. Receive

"We need to give each other the space to grow, to be ourselves, to exercise our diversity. We need to give each other space so that we may both give and receive such beautiful things as ideas, openness, dignity, joy, healing, and inclusion."

—Max de Pree

Receive . . .

1. **Meet, greet or bid welcome;**
2. **Get or accept.**

Why Receive? By opening your heart to gratefully receive the kindness, generosity, and service of others, you not only enjoy the benefits of their consideration, but you also allow them the gift of giving.

Are you comfortable and willing to be of service to others, but find it difficult to receive the same in return? Are you quick to give, but resist receiving, even when you need the help? Your ability to receive not only opens the space for great things to enter your life, it also returns a gift of grace to the giver.

Refusal and Rejection

The statement, "It is better to give than to receive" is a confusing and ridiculous theory, without without explanation. Giving and receiving require participation in both directions to make the circle complete. It is a reciprocal interaction requiring mutual generosity, respect, appreciation—and humility. It is a reciprocal interaction requiring mutual generosity, respect, appreciation—and humility.

However, while many people will give you the shirt off their backs, they will never ask for help. Is it because they do not want to impose or inconvenience anyone? Or is it possible that they will feel obligated to return the favor? Or perhaps it's pride that gets in the way.

We also experience this rejection from people whom we attempt to compliment or celebrate. Why would someone reject praise or refuse a kind deed when it is offered with sincerity, love, support, and generosity?

Is it because they feel undeserving and unworthy? Is it because it makes them uncomfortable or embarrassed to receive singled-out attention, even though it is positive? Do they feel it makes them appear less humble, or a flattery seeker or someone who likes the spotlight?

Regardless, we've all probably been on both ends of the "giving and receiving" cycle, and felt uncomfortable with the response we got, or the response we may have given. Even if it is uncomfortable for you to receive, soften the rejection by kindly responding with a smile, and a simple "Thank you."

5 Things to Receive Graciously. Be Willing to . . .

1. Receive help.
2. Receive gifts.
3. Receive kindness.
4. Receive feedback.
5. Receive compliments.

Create the Space to Receive

Open your heart to possibilities, open your mind to opportunities, and open your imagination to creativity, and you will attract amazing blessings just waiting to be received! Once you consciously decide that you are open to give and receive graciously and gratefully, an abundance of good things will rush in to meet you.

69. Rebound

"The ability to bounce back after a setback is probably the single most important trait an entrepreneurial venture can possess."

—Ricard Branson

Rebound . . .

1. **Resiliency, reaction;**
2. **Spring back from force or impact;**
3. **Recover from illness or discouragement.**

Why Rebound? Life will inevitably hand us unexpected setbacks, hardships, and failures that we must find a way to prevail over.

The Key to Your Resilience

The world is going through such incredible change that my program *Shift, Shed & Shine: How to Thrive in Times of Change* has been among my most requested. I was recently hired by the Social Security Administration in Washington, DC, to deliver the program to empower the employees with tools for resilience. You can only imagine the changes they are enduring with budget cuts, heavy regulation, increasing workloads—and their exploding customer base with the baby boomers hitting retirement age. No stress there, right?

During one of my programs, a participant raised her hand and basically shared, "I have always been a resilient person, however, life has worn me down. I have been knocked down so many times, that I'm not springing back as fast as I used to."

Isn't this the epitome of how important it is for us to nurture ourselves and find healthy ways to bounce back when challenges hit hard?

Bounce-ability Factor

Your bounce-ability factor will help determine your resilience in how you handle setbacks, adversity, and challenge. Three light-hearted resilience styles are illustrated through the following analogies:

1. The egg . . .

It spends all its time begging you, "Don't drop me! Please don't drop me." Do you know people who refuse to try new things or leave their comfort zones for fear of being hurt or pushed to the breaking point—*where they might become cracked?* Being safe and careful is their first concern, because they fear that difficulties or setbacks will shatter them.

2. The orange . . .

It expects to get dropped. And when it is, it doesn't even bruise. It even rolls. It looks fine on the outside, but on the inside it is soft, pulpy juice. Do you know people who take the hit, but seem to absorb the shock and the heaviness all within themselves? They might seem and look fine, but tend to carry the burden of the pain alone, which feeds their bitterness, or the grudges they hold. Perhaps they lash out at others, due to staying stuck and alone in their suffering—holding in the pain that others cannot see.

3. The bouncy ball . . .

As you drop it, it hits the ground and joyfully bounces 4, 6, even 10 feet high, screaming "Yiippeeeee!" For others it may not seem real; their innate ability to rebound so effortlessly. It is the hardness of the surface which actually propels them higher and farther. They seize the opportunity to adapt to the circumstances and use it as a learning opportunity to fly high and discover new places in life.

Which Style Do You Gravitate More Toward?

Pun intended! Not everyone bounces back at the same rate from adversity because we all have different coping skills, life experiences, beliefs, and attitudes. Simply becoming aware of your own resilience style will help you be more mindful when you choose your response. Building your resilience will give you more bounce-ability—to effectively rebound—and enable you to recover more quickly.

In sports, a rebound occurs when a ball bounces back from a hard surface. When the ball hits the backboard, it gets bounced in a new direction which keeps the game going. And in life, we all want to stay in the game. No matter the direction, we want to improve our ability, workout to become strong, and keep our ball in play. Life provides the workout—though some may doubt it, each one of us can learn to become that bouncy ball!

When you hit hard tough stuff, do you crack, roll on or feel flattened because of it—or bounce in a new direction to keep living, loving, moving, and growing? Are you quick to rebound or slow to recover?

Make it a habit to focus on "what is," good, not what isn't. I offer this one skill to help strengthen your rebound, but I'm happy to individually coach if you want to play more!

"Resilience isn't a single skill. It's a variety of skills and coping mechanisms. To bounce back from bumps in the road as well as failures, you should focus on emphasizing the positive."
—Jean Chatzky

70. $\mathcal{R}e$-emerge

"That is the real spiritual awakening, when something emerges from within you that is deeper than who you thought you were. So, the person is still there, but one could almost say that something more powerful shines through the person."

—Eckhart Tolle

$\mathcal{R}e$-emerge . . .

1. **Make a comeback, reappear;**
2. **Come into sight or prominence once again;**
3. **Rise again as from an inferior or unfortunate condition.**

Why Re-emerge? Something may be at work deep inside you that is greater than you realize; seek it, acknowledge it, release it, and allow your light to shine in the world.

Transformations Revealed

"Move that bus!" This statement is from one of my favorite TV shows, "Extreme Makeovers." It's no longer on, but they would take a family in need and renovate, rebuild, restore, and renew their home to be bigger, better, and more beautiful than ever. The families were given the gift of a dream home through the love, generosity, kindness, and donations of volunteers and sponsors. Once their home was ready, it re-emerged as a dream come true.

Similarly, it is impressive to see how people work hard to transform their lives, their bodies, and their relationships to become the best version of themselves. Before and after photos illustrate their re-emergence as if to reintroduce themselves to the world. Release the layers that weigh you down and hold you back. There are things within you that can come to light, surface, and materialize. Release the past and see what might re-emerge as you prepare to begin the next chapter in your life. Be open to recognizing something greater than yourself is at work that can emerge from within you.

From What Can You Re-emerge?

- Re-emerge from failure and find success.
- Re-emerge from setbacks and become victorious.
- Re-emerge from heartbreak and love again.
- Re-emerge from depression and be happy again.
- Re-emerge from the shadows and live in the light again.
- Re-emerge from isolation and solitude to engage with others.

Re-emerge Victorious

"When people endure a traumatic event, they are either defeated or made stronger. On Sept. 11, I told New Yorkers, 'I want you to emerge stronger from this.' My words were partially a hope and partially an observation that people in New York City handle big things better than little things. I could not be more proud of the way my city responded."

—Rudy Giuliani

Have you ever travelled through an emotionally dark and painful valley which felt like the walls were surrounding you on all sides? Yet, as you continued to forge through, you could see the light at the end of the tunnel? And as you stepped into the light, did you re-emerge wiser, stronger, and more resilient than you were before? There is much to be gained from successfully navigating through change and re-emerging on the other side victorious.

71. Rejuvenate

"Do whatever rejuvenates you. It might be a cooking class, cocktails with the girls, or just private time with the hubby. We all have our moments where we run out of steam because we've given everything we've got to everyone else. Whoever decided that was a good thing? It's not. Everyone needs to refuel."

—Jada Pinkett Smith

Rejuvenate . . .

1. **Make young again;**
2. **Restore youthful vigor;**
3. **Make fresh or new again.**

Why Rejuvenate? Make life more enjoyable and invigorating. Maximize your qualities and boost your energy for excellence—every day.

Rejuvenation is a cleansing word that conjures images of jumping into a pool of cool water on a hot summer day. It refreshes our senses, washes away the remains of the day, and renews our energy from head to toe. It even makes us feel younger!

Rejuvenation happens when you intentionally make the time to self-nurture. The result is to spring back and spring forth—revitalized. Turn on your favorite music and discover the joy of movement, play, and dance to shift your energy to a higher vibration.

When we do not make rejuvenation a part of our self-care, our reserves can become depleted. When there is little left within us, it is hard to graciously provide for others who count on us—most of us know this all too well.

Rejuvenation happens when you do not have the resources to draw upon for resilience, you might become more vulnerable to anxiety, depression, destructive temptations, and negative emotions. To avoid and overcome these unhealthy states, find ways to rejuvenate and renew. Make the most of the wellness practices that have been proven to work for you—or try something new.

5 Ways for You to Rejuvenate

1. Get plenty of rest.
2. Detox your mind, body, and spirit from stress, contaminants, and unhealthy living.
3. Eat healthy foods and drink a lot of water.
4. Watch mindless shows filled with love, happiness, and laughter.
5. Take a spa day for luxurious indulgence.
6. Spend time in laughter and fun with a good friend.

Does This Sound Familiar?

If I asked you, "When was the last time you went on a vacation?" your response might be: "It depends on what your definition of a vacation is."

I might add: "It's when you go somewhere for five nights without a computer."

In this scenario, many people answer, "Well, I guess that means I have never been on a vacation."

In the particular case I'm thinking of, to take a real vacation, the woman left town for five nights. She flew to Atlanta, rented a car, and went gallivanting by herself to play, explore, and discover to her heart's content. She later shared with me that it was life changing and powerful. Before this, she had had no idea how badly she needed to unplug and recharge, until she created the time, space, and place to fully rejuvenate.

A Zest for Life

My friend Lysianne Unruh runs the company Time to Thrive Coaching (www.timetothrivecoaching.com) where she works as a happiness strategist and empowerment coach helping women in transition turn these times of change into a source of power and opportunity.

One reason her clients enroll in her coaching is because they have lost their juicy enthusiasm and want to get their zest back.

Lysianne shares a delightful metaphor for zest. She says, "It's an enlivening pop of citrus-y goodness when bits of lime, lemon or orange peel get added to a recipe. It doesn't take much—a tablespoon or two—to transform a dessert or cocktail."

She continues, "Zesty people are like that too. Their enthusiasm and energy infuse liveliness into whatever situation or task is at hand. It doesn't take much—usually one laughing, smiling, energetic person can elevate the energy in a room."

A zestful spirit and enthusiastic attitude can rejuvenate not only the person who exudes it, but everyone's whose lives are touched. Seek ways to create 'jolts of joy' and add zest to your life for true rejuvenation.

72. Reaccelerate

"Amplifying what is great within you will accelerate your life faster than fixing what you think 'limits' you."

—Brendan Burchard

Reaccelerate . . .

1. **Increase velocity or speed;**
2. **Go faster, gain momentum.**

Why Reaccelerate? When we lose momentum and stop moving toward our dreams—or are unable to function normally in our day—it's time to pick ourselves up, turn our engines on, and get going!

Slow Down to Go Fast

As I emphasized in the last chapter, sometimes you will find it necessary to de-accelerate when life gets crazy or veers out of control—to rejuvenate. Slowing down will provide you with the opportunity to make time to review, regroup, reroute, and decide how to turn the corner or change direction. While slowing down comes with incredible benefits to reduce stress, if you stay there too long, you may become stuck or stranded. When everything comes to a grinding halt, it can be hard to generate the energy to get rolling again—which can allow inertia to set in.

Fighting Inertia

A plane on the ground requires more energy, fuel, and effort to get it up and in the air than it takes to sustain its flight. The same can be said about going to the gym. Getting off the couch and driving there is usually harder than the workout you receive once you arrive. Why do we tend to gravitate to the line of least resistance? It is easy to get stuck in inertia if we don't exercise the sheer will and determination to bust through it, increase our speed, and get moving.

Shifting Gears

Successfully shifting gears to get moving again requires desire, synchronization, coordination, and a change of pace, whether starting off slow or fast. It is your ability to respond to circumstances to ensure controlled acceleration. Mindful awareness of both yourself and your environment will assist your emotional intelligence to guide you as to the level of acceleration that is needed.

Building Momentum

"It is never the size of your problem that is the problem.
It's a lack of momentum."
—John Maxwell

To build up your speed and create momentum, do you need to be pushed or pulled? Sometimes, it is simply a matter of shaking up your routine to get things rolling in the right direction.

In *The Compound Effect: Jumpstart Your Income, Your Life, Your Success,* Darren Hardy recommends building momentum by consistently performing a series of smart and small steps. While a consistent routine of positive habits will help lead you to success, you will get farther faster by shaking up your day. Do something different. Try something new.

7 Ways to Build Momentum

"The rhythm of daily action aligned with your goals creates the momentum that separates dreamers from super-achievers."
—Darren Hardy

1. Create a morning routine; wake up early, start strong.
2. Set realistic goals and track your benchmarks.
3. Create a series of successful endings, not beginnings.
4. Acknowledge and affirm small contributions.
5. Focus on solutions more than problems.
6. Have positive expectations for probable wins.
7. Focus on strengths rather than weaknesses.

Reaccelerate to your heart's content, because . . .

"There are no speed limits on the road to success."
—David W. Johnson

73. Reharmonize

"Happiness is not a matter of intensity but of balance,
order, rhythm and harmony."
—Thomas Merton

Reharmonize . . .

1. **Recreate agreement, order, congruity, accord;**
2. **A pleasing arrangement of parts.**

Why Reharmonize? Bringing various qualities together in harmony will create music rather than noise, bringing peace, calm, and delight.

In the rhythm of life, perfect harmony is bliss, yet challenging to achieve on a regular basis. Due to that, we can get used to being "out of tune," with one or more people, and go on as if everything is perfectly fine.

To achieve the perfect pitch is quite a skill. It has to be a priority. One has to know the difference.

Have you ever seen a barber shop quartet sing without background music? They will blow into a tuner to get the right pitch before they even begin to sing. By starting with the right pitch, their diverse voices are able to come together in perfect harmony to optimize their performance.

My son, Nick, who plays the guitar beautifully, does something similar. Every time he sits down to play, he will open the guitar tuner app on his cell phone and tune the strings so that bad keys do not lead him astray and compromise his experience and sound. Tuning up results in better outcomes.

Dreadful Discord

Our life, and the people and circumstances in it, can sometimes sound like a musical orchestra warming up. As each musician plays his or her individual instrument in preparation for the concert, the resulting sound is a cacophony of chaos and conflict. Without regard to the screeching sounds around them, they may be oblivious to the painful discord being inflicted on the listener.

Once they all come together in unison, however, they are then able to create extraordinary music with beautiful sounds. When they practice re-harmonization, all parts come together for good and create incredible beauty for the listener.

When elements in your life are out of tune, in conflict, or clashing against each other, it is time to tune-in, tune-up, and re-harmonize.

Reharmonizing Involves . . .

- Turning your "listening ear" to the other person.
- Modifying your own chords to harmonize with the other person.
- Understanding your own inner workings.
- Striving to deepen understanding of yourself, to deepen understanding between you and the other person.
- Recognizing two instruments are different, yet when reharmonized, make sweet music together.

"The requirements for our evolution have changed. Survival is no longer sufficient. Our evolution now requires us to develop spiritually— to become emotionally aware and make responsible choices. It requires us to align ourselves with the values of the soul— harmony, cooperation, sharing, and reverence for life."
—Gary Zukav

74. Restrengthen

"If we strive to strengthen our body now; to overcome our faults; to cultivate new virtues; the Sun of our next life will rise under much more auspicious conditions than those under which we now live, and thus we may truly rule our stars and master our fate."

—Max Heindel

Restrengthen . . .

1. To be fortified, made stronger or more powerful

Why Restrengthen? Fortifying your personal strength, potency, and power boosts your confidence, energy, and courage to boldly navigate change and transformation.

Even a life lived well uses our resources to such a degree that it can weaken many areas which were once strong. Simple wear and tear may tire us and take its toll to the point that we need to be re-fortified if we wish to continue performing at higher levels.

14 Areas to Restrengthen for Success

1. Your body
2. Your mind
3. Your spirit
4. Your skills
5. Your resolve
6. Your resilience
7. Your values
8. Your discipline
9. Your resilience
10. Your confidence
11. Your relationships
12. Your commitment
13. Your capability for compassion
14. Your emotional intelligence

75. Reconnect

"Spend time with family and friends. Relationships are sacred, for in them we come to know ourselves deeply, to heal and be healed. And relationships require time and attention. Even the people you love will grow resentful if you take that love for granted."

—Joan Borysenko

Reconnect . . .

1. **Re-establish a bond of communication or emotion;**
2. **Meet or come into contact again after a long absence.**

Why Reconnect? Connection is one of our greatest needs and desires as social animals—to progress and prosper, we need to feel acceptance, inclusion, fulfilment, and emotional safety.

Reconnect with Yourself

"We need time to defuse, to contemplate. Just as in sleep our brains relax and give us dreams, so at some time in the day we need to disconnect, reconnect, and look around us."

—Laurie Colwin

Reconnect with who you truly are and what you really want, rather than letting the outside world determine it for you. Reconnect with your purpose and your passion to confirm if your actions are helping you to achieve it.

Reconnect to what makes you happy and brings you joy. If there is something that used to make you happy which you may have stopped doing, do it again. Seek to find deeper meaning and significance rather than living on the surface, skimming along.

Reconnect with Others

Reconnect with the ones you love by being authentic, being vulnerable, healing hurts, communicating well, and nurturing your relationships. Remember to laugh and have fun. And reconnect with old friends whom you miss, but never see. Reconnect with the special people in your life with whom you have shared some of the best times in your life. Feel the joy!

It is no wonder that Facebook, LinkedIn and other social media platforms are so successful, considering the world's driving need to feel connected with others.

Whether it is to celebrate the good times or offer a shoulder to lean on in the bad times, your relationships are essential for happiness and well-being. Connecting with others gives you a sense of inclusion, connection, interaction, safety, and community. Your vibe attracts your tribe, and so if you want to attract positive and healthy relationships, be the one who promotes getting together! Staying connected and getting reconnected feeds the flow of goodness which empowers our humanity.

Reconnect to Source

"If you look to your past or even your present to see why you are here or what your purpose is, you may get stuck in a limited view of yourself. Instead, look beyond your years here on earth, reconnect with the divine, and bring forth your soul's legacy into the present moment."

— Debbie Ford

Take time to commune with your highest and best understanding of God. Within you, there is a *Knowing* that you can access at all times. To do so, you must be quiet and still. Go into the silence. Tap into the Source from which all things come, beyond self, beyond time. Surrender into it. Let go. Allow. Be. Each time you reconnect with what many call "Universal Love," others call God, you will emerge renewed.

When Disconnection is Your Best Option

If you find you are attracting dysfunctional, negative, unhealthy people into your life, pay attention to what signals you're sending to see if that explains what is bringing them to you. At any moment, you can change your signals and change that connection.

To live a wholesome life and renew with joy, you may need to identify the people who are simply not good for you. Your disconnection from them may be essential for your own self-preservation and emotional safety.

If there is someone in your life who makes you feel bad about yourself, is mean, rude, abusive, disrespectful, sarcastic, disloyal, or dismissive, it may be time for you to disconnect. Getting caught in their drama can bring untold suffering. Sometimes it's just a matter of refusing to participate in their crazy-making. *Not my monkeys, not my circus.*

What happens when you do not have the luxury of disconnecting from these exhausting people? What can you do if you are related to, married to, or have to work with a person like this? Take measures to protect your self-respect, self-esteem, and well-being.

Whether it is setting boundaries, having a crucial conversation, practicing involved detachment, minimizing contact, getting outside support via a 12-Step group like Al Anon or a counselor, or avoiding them altogether, take control and stand in your power, then choose how you can best respond.

Psychological Thriving

In his book, *The Power of the Other . . . The Startling Effects Others Have On Us from the Bedroom to the Boardroom and Beyond and What to Do About It,* Dr. Henry Cloud names four levels of connection for human interaction and engagement.

1. Disconnection
2. Bad Connection
3. Fake-Good Connection
4. Real Connection

He dives deep into sharing why "Real Connection" is the only place where true, authentic, psychological thriving happens. While his model is amazingly simple, it gives you a profound tool with which to measure the levels of connection you have with everyone and everything in your life. I highly recommend it.

Meaningful Levels

"I believe that our success is in direct correlation to how we impact and influence other people. And the secret to having more influence is not in our ability to communicate, but to connect. Master the art of connection, and you will go places you never thought possible.
—Kelly Swanson

It is one thing to communicate, but something entirely different to connect on a deep and meaningful level. Reconnection is not just about being reunited and brought back together again, it is about connecting in a more intimate and authentic fashion.

8 Tips for Making Meaningful Connections

1. Build trust and rapport.
2. Be personable and friendly.
3. Be genuinely interested in others.
4. Become a discovery expert and ask questions.
5. Take the initiative to be an inviter, the liker, and the host.
6. Find commonality, camaraderie, and shared interests.
7. Make others feel valued and important.
8. Use humor to diffuse tension, shift energy, and feed laughter.

Powerful Practices for Deepening Bonds

Relationships are continually shifting and being redefined. In their book, *Friendship Interrupted,* my friend Judy Dippel and her co-author Debra Whiting Alexander, Ph.D., write, "At the core of every important and meaningful friendship is a close relationship that adjusts and compensates as needed." They continue to advise, "To stay healthy, relationships require plenty of attention and commitment." To reconnect and make relationships more meaningful, they encourage you to practice:

- **Patience:** Patience in action can be a tremendous gift.
- **Encouragement:** It can rekindle hope and soothe the spirit.
- **Acceptance:** Genuine acceptance brings grace and mercy.
- **Respect:** Allows you to interact and engage appropriately.
- **Loyalty:** Faithful friends are unwavering.
- **Laughter:** Stimulates a natural sense of camaraderie.
- **Service:** A thriving friendship can't help but produce good works, and in doing so strengthens bonds.

76. Reimagine

"I remember the past, and I learn from it. I rejoice and celebrate the present, and I re-imagine the future. Now is the moment that never ends."

—Deepak Chopra

Reimagine . . .

1. **Imagine again or anew, especially for forming a new concept;**
2. **Form a new mental image of something which is not actually present to the senses.**

Why Reimagine? Reimagining will enable you to go beyond the edge of your current reality and expand your vision, possibilities, and understanding.

Reimagine Your Vision

Re-imagination is the birthplace for renewed vision and change. Your imagination is one of the most valuable talents you have, and deserves your full attention. Imagining how you want to live your life is one thing, but connecting your imagination to a visual representation will give you exactly the traction you need to make it a reality. Visual imagery allows you the opportunity to feel, touch, taste, and embrace what it would be like for your dreams to come true.

Imagine setting goals in every area of your life to fulfill your heart's desires, and then connect each goal to a visual image to see it accomplished. It is a powerful way to retrain the brain to expect and manifest success.

Proven methods for visualization include vision boards, vision books, mind-mapping, and creative brainstorming. Begin connecting your imagination with visual symbols and it will make your re-imagination process fruitful and fulfilling.

Reimagine the Possibilities

What would you do today if you knew you couldn't fail and success was guaranteed? Answering this brilliant question will require you to move beyond your current reality, remove failure from the equation, and actively engage your imagination. Why not?

With imagining all things as being possible, how would you like for your life to look 5, 10, and 15 years from now? Reimagine what it would look like if your wildest dreams could come to fruition.

My friend Dan Burrus is a global futurist, international speaker, best-selling author, and a consultant to businesses, governments, and organizations across the world. Dan's platform has been enriched by his ability to help others imagine beyond our current reality and discover trends which can predict and change an individual's future.

In his book, *Flash Foresight . . . How to See the Invisible and Do the Impossible,* he defines flash foresight as having a "sudden burst of insight about the future that produces a new and radically different way of doing something that will open up invisible opportunities and solve seemingly impossible problems before they happen." As a teacher, one of his greatest joys is detonating idea bombs in the minds of his audiences, and it all begins with each individual's imagination.

Re-imaginers

Re-imaginers are those special people among us who use their imaginations without allowing fear, judgment, failure, or the opinions of others to stand in their way. They have the rare ability to step into their imaginations, play around a while, and bring forth brilliant and creative expressions in their work, their play, and in their business.

Re-imaginers Include:

- Artists
- Risk Takers
- Game changers
- Innovators
- Inventors
- Problem solvers
- Riders
- Storytellers
- Actors
- Painters

When Imagination Goes to the Dark Side

"Since most of our fears are based on dark imaginings, it is vital for us to dwell on our magnificent obsessions and desired results—to look at where we want to go, as opposed to that troubled place where we may have been or may still be hiding."

—Denis Waitley

Be aware that your imagination can work in your favor or against you. Have you known people who imagine the worst, and as a result, that is exactly what they attract? When they imagine they will be an epic failure, their negative expectation becomes their reality. When they imagine they are going to get hurt in a relationship, they do. Their run-away imaginations become detrimental to their health and well-being. Their imagination prevents them from living a fabulous, adventurous, rewarding life.

Just as your imagination can be the ball and chain which imprisons you in fear and resistance, it can also be the key which unlocks the gate for you to run free and live an extraordinary life. It is vital to know the difference.

What Can You Reimagine?

- Reimagine being pain free.
- Reimagine having vibrant and sustainable energy.
- Reimagine having mental clarity and acuity.
- Reimagine doing the impossible.
- Reimagine living the ultimate lifestyle.
- Reimagine financial freedom and prosperity.
- Reimagine a career where your work is your passion.
- Reimagine a happy home and a loving family.
- Reimagine being surrounded by family and friends who love, accept, and adore you.
- Reimagine having the financial abundance to make a difference in the lives of many.
- Reimagine living in a peaceful world without hunger, hate, or cruelty.

Pick one—allow your positive imagination to start there! Three of my favorite books for "Re-imagining" which you might enjoy are:

- *The Art of Possibility* by Benjamin and Rosamund Stone Zanders
- *The Magic of Thinking Big* by David J. Schwartz
- *Jumpstart Your Brain* by Doug Hall and David Wecker

"PRETENDING HAS ITS REWARDS—The mind cannot distinguish between what is real and what is make-believe. Perception has nothing to do with reality. What we imagine can be as real to us as reality itself. Consequently, the way we act in real life can be determined beforehand by imagining a situation, then imagining the best possible action we could take."

—Ellen Kriedman

77. Rejoice

"I want to be thoroughly used up when I die, for the harder I work, the more I live. I rejoice in life for its own sake."

—George Bernard Shaw

Rejoice . . .

1. **To be glad, take delight in;**
2. **Feel or show great happiness, pleasure, joy, elation, jubilation, exuberance, celebration.**

Why Rejoice? Living in a spirit of gratitude and celebration not only attracts more good to flow your way, but it also shifts your being into a state of bliss—which is a wonderful way to experience life.

Make the Choice to Rejoice

"Be content with what you have; rejoice in the way things are. When you realize there is nothing lacking, the whole world belongs to you."

—Lao Tzu

The present moment is all you truly have. Your past is over and your future has yet to occur. Every moment of happiness and joy is occurring in the NOW.

Rejoicing is grounded in gratitude, with a keen appreciation for yourself, others, your abundance, and the beauty around you. Without an *attitude of gratitude*, it is all too easy to get caught up in:

- Focusing on scarcity rather than prosperity.
- Focusing on what is not working rather than what is.
- Focusing on your weaknesses, rather than your strengths.

- Taking your blessings for granted.
- Feeling a right of entitlement.

Even in the worst of times, you can find something to be grateful for, but you must seek it to see it, no matter the difficulty of the circumstance. In his book, *Man's Search for Meaning*, Victor Frankl describes how as a concentration camp prisoner during the Holocaust, he was able to find purpose and meaning in his circumstances. Finding something to be grateful for gave him a reason to keep living.

While the changes in our lives are not so tragic or extreme as his, we can still lose sight of what matters most and fail to feel grateful. It is uplifting to rejoice in both the small and the large, the ordinary and the extraordinary.

12 Blessings to Rejoice In

1. Free will
2. Being alive
3. Being safe
4. Being well
5. Being free
6. Having a family
7. Having friends
8. Abundance of food
9. Modern conveniences
10. Technological advances
11. Unlimited opportunities
12. Life-saving medicine and health care

I hope you will receive this gift—because to rejoice in something is a gift you give yourself. It's a choice to see and appreciate this very moment. It's free—and it's freeing.

"Whatever we are waiting for—peace of mind, contentment, grace, the inner awareness of simple abundance—it will surely come to us, but only when we are ready to receive it with an open and grateful heart."

— Sarah Ban Breathnach

Results & Rewards

The changes in your life can bring determination or doubt, joy or pain, victory or defeat, confidence or fear, and security or risk. Regardless of the meanings you assign to change, when you embrace it as a consistent reality and fortify yourself with tools for resilience, you will be more empowered to flourish. *Release the Power of Re³* will help you create positive change for better results and lasting rewards.

Review, Redo, and Renew to:

- Achieve your goals.
- Shine to your true potential.
- Design and live a life you love.
- Inspire the best in yourself and others.
- Shift your mindset to embrace change.
- Strengthen and invest in your relationships.
- Move through adversity, trials, and challenge.
- Open your mind to new ideas and possibilities.
- Get you unstuck to start moving in the right direction.
- Help you bounce back faster after being knocked down.
- Shed limiting beliefs and values that no longer serve you.
- Gain clarity and discern details to optimize your outcomes.
- Improve your performance, productivity, and effectiveness.
- Transform communication, collaboration, and engagement.
- Clear the path and remove obstacles that stand in your way.
- Be proactive in taking the necessary steps to move from transition to transformation.

Pearls of Wisdom

Like the grain of sand which imposes itself in an oyster, the changes in your life can be irritating, annoying, uncomfortable, and unpredictable. To protect itself from harm, the resilient oyster will coat the irritant in layers of nacre. As the layers grow and a pearl is formed, an iridescent glow is created. The oyster has taken what might have first appeared to be an intrusion and used it to create something entirely new. No grit, no pearl. How can you coat or frame the changes in your life to create something valuable and beautiful too?

Finding Gifts in the Pain

Change is inevitable, but growth is optional. Every experience you have can bring you lessons when you make the time and effort to find them. Even if they are lessons with which you could have lived without, seek the opportunity to find deeper meaning. Even if it was a mistake or an epic failure, you now know how not to do something in the future. Many of your greatest life lessons will come from your most difficult challenges. Catch the lesson and release the pain whenever possible.

Shine like a Diamond

A diamond is one of the most resilient and enduring creations found on earth. Beginning as a lump of coal, it endures immense pressure and heat to reach it highest potential. Rather than being crushed under the grind, it evolves over time into a beautiful and rare treasure. As in our own lives, we will endure pressure, challenge, and change. As you overcome and conquer, may the changes of your life transform you for the good. Be brilliant, be resilient, and let your priceless value shine!

Your Rich and Resilient Treasures

By learning skills for resilience, gathering pearls of wisdom along the way, finding gifts in the pain, and persevering through the challenges of life, you will be blessed with rich resources for living life well and thriving in times of change.

I sincerely hope that *Release the Power of Re³* has given you new tools, insights, and ideas to do just that.

Thank you for taking the time to read this book, and whether you gained a few pearls of wisdom or many, I encourage you to share it with others. You never know when one idea can shift the trajectory of a person's life and change it for the better.

Consider keeping it handy for reference when you are faced with a shift, a change, or a new goal so that we can be there to help you on your journey.

Please stay in touch through www.SusanSpeaks.com and keep us in mind if we may ever be of service for speaking, training, and coaching.

May you always embrace change with optimism, positive expectations, and resilience.

Warmly,

Susan Young

About The Author

Susan YOUNG
Change Expert
Keynote Speaker
Leadership Trainer
www.SusanSpeaks.com

Susan runs the speaking and training firm, **Susan Young International.** She speaks for organizations who want to leverage the power of change to improve positivity, engagement, and performance. As a leadership trainer, she designs and delivers game-changing experiences which help people get laser-focused to achieve their goals.

With charismatic humor, a passion for the human spirit, and the real-life tools people need today, Susan breaks the challenge of change and the process of transformation down into practical strategies that help even the most resistant people take immediate action to find the balance, joy, and life-affirming moments that make engaging in the world worthwhile.

For more than two decades, Susan has studied, learned, and lived what it takes to thrive through change and be resilient. With a Master's Degree in Human Performance Technology, she has dedicated her professional career to helping people move from TRANSITION TO TRANSFORMATION.

Susan is the proud mother of twins Nick and Ally. To celebrate the birth of her first grandbaby, Jace, she jumped out of an airplane over Oahu. She lives in Madison, Wisconsin with her life mate and love, Daniel Futch.

Acknowledgements

Thank you to the special people who helped me make this dream come true. You were the wind beneath my wings to make it fly and I am grateful.

Daniel Futch, My Champion

Thank you to the man I love, my life-mate and partner Daniel Futch, for believing in me and providing me with the space, place, freedom, love, and commitment to help me live my dream. I love you, baby.

Elizabeth Dixon, My Editor

Thank you to my brilliant sister, Elizabeth Dixon, for helping me enrich my message by editing every word, concept, and idea. Your loving hand and profound guidance has made my writing come to life so that I may bring my message of hope, change, and resilience to the world.

Cheri Neal, My Muse

Thank you to Cheri Neal for being my muse. With my outline in one hand and my audio recorder in the other, we would talk on the phone while I walked in the woods. We passionately discussed every topic and our dynamic conversations helped me create rapid fire content with profound meaning and impact.

Kendra Cagle, My Graphic Designer

Thank you to Kendra Cagle for your extraordinary talent and unlimited creativity in bringing my vision to fruition. You are a cherished member of my team and I cannot imagine where my books, professional branding, and digital presence would be without you.

My Angel Posse

Thank you to Ann Cullison, Marjorie Jane Chandley, George Chandley, Jane Cullison Vosser, Christine Collins, Farrell Hendricks, Rachel Dixon, Sarah Jane Klump, Maya Boone, Jordan Stearns, Tina Hallis, Amy Tolbert, Deborah SuZan, Judy Dippel, and Adrianne Machina for your contributions and feedback. Your love, support, encouragement, and friendship mean the world to me.

When the main book, *The Art of First Impressions for Positive Impact,* was finally finished, it was almost 100,00 words and over 400 pages! With 8 content-rich chapters that could make complete stand-alone topics, I decided to showcase each one and give it its own book! In your busy life with everything vying for your attention, I wanted to make it easy for you to enjoy this valuable content in whatever form worked best for you. Whether you read the main book, one of the 8 small books, or all nine, these valuable lessons are timeless, true, and ready for you. Please visit Amazon.com or SusanSpeaks.com to buy your copies today.

Resources

Quotes:

The Bible
www.brainyquote.com
www.searchquotes.com
www.worldofquotes.com
www.goodreads.com

Definitions:

www.google.com
www.wikihow.com
www.vocabulary.com
www.en.wikipedia.org
www.urbandictionary.com
www.merriam-webster.com
www.collinsdictionary.com
www.thefreedictionary.com
www.learnersdictionary.com
www.oxforddictionaries.com

Made in the USA
Columbia, SC
04 March 2019